UFOs
and How to See them

UFOs

and How to See them

JENNY RANDLES

BARNES
&NOBLE
BOOKS
NEW YORK

This edition published by
Barnes & Noble, Inc. by
arrangement with Sterling Publishing Co., Inc.
1997 Barnes & Noble Books

ISBN 0-7607-0549-6

Designed by The R & B Partnership
Phototypeset by Intype, London
Colour reproduction by J. Film Process, Bangkok
Printed by Midas, Hong Kong

CONTENTS

INTRODUCTION

THIS IS not just a book about UFO sightings. It is designed to be used by anyone who has seen something strange in the sky or – indeed – anyone who would *like* to see something strange but does not know where to start. If you have ever wanted to join the millions from almost every country on earth who believe they have spotted a UFO – then this book is specially written to help you in that task.

After an introduction to the history of the UFO mystery, ranging over thousands of years, we enter the main heart of the book.

Firstly, there is a section for all those who think they may have already seen a UFO. Using our unique picture and text reference system you can test your own encounter against the many different phenomena for which it can be mistaken. After that you will have a fair idea whether you have really seen a UFO or will need to keep on trying.

If your sighting does not match up, don't despair. The rest of the book is full of tips on how to increase your chances of having a genuine close encounter.

You will find advice on how to organize a sky-watch, the best way to take photographs and capture that elusive evidence that might convince the world that UFOs are real – and what you should do if you are lucky enough to spot something truly extraordinary. There is even an observer's identi-kit guide to the most common UFO types so that you can check what you saw against what we have discovered about the phenomenon.

In Part Two of the book we have put together a complete survey of the world's most UFO-haunted locations – what we are calling hot spots. Using this section of the book, you will learn where to go to have maximum opportunity of finding UFOs and what you might expect to see if you do go there.

UFOs are the greatest mystery of the space age. If proof can be established it may change the world. Anyone can get that proof and solve the mystery . . . Are you ready for the adventure?

Part I Background

1 THE UFO STORY

1000 BC:
The First Witness

ACCORDING TO the Old Testament of the Bible, the prophet Ezekiel was one of the first human beings to have a close encounter. But is this graphic recollection in *Ezekiel, Chapter 1* a vain attempt to describe the indescribable – or little more than a dream?

The prophet writes of a 'whirlwind' and 'great cloud' with 'fire infolding itself', which churned up the desert sands as it descended. It then manifested as 'a wheel in the middle of a wheel' and fired 'lightning' bolts to the earth. With the craft shining like polished metal in the sunlight the tale became a 'contact', when strange beings were seen inside. The voice of God reputedly then spoke of peace and goodwill, leaving the startled witness with a paranormal ability to see into the future.

Thousands of years later episodes almost exactly like this still take place. Of course, today the witnesses to such a phenomenon struggle to describe it to stubborn disbelievers and may also be left with vague, confusing messages or paranormal effects. They are not considered prophets who have conversed with the Almighty. The world sees them as deluded or some of the select few who have held a meeting with aliens from the stars.

The parallels are appropriate. The questions they pose unanswered.

Ezekiel's spaceship is almost as hotly debated as modern UFO encounters. It has been hailed as proof that spacecraft from another world touched down in the Middle East or that sightings are an hallucination. In 1991 a physicist investigating strange circles forming in crop fields even sug-

UFOs are not a new phenomenon. This medieval illustration from Switzerland describes what was seen on 7 August 1566 at Basel. Strange lights have always appeared in the sky. Today we simply know them as UFOs.

The first photograph taken of a UFO. An astronomer at a Mexican observatory snapped these objects crossing the face of the sun using a camera attached to his telescope. That was in August 1883.

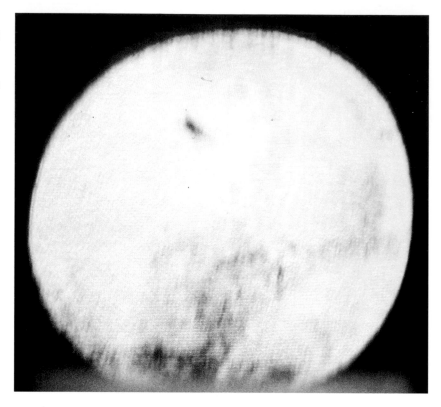

gested that the prophet may have seen a whirling cloud of electrified air that he believes may be the cause of this modern-day mystery.

The Ezekiel story has been hijacked by the experts to establish their own version of the truth. That is how it is in the world of UFOlogy.

AUGUST 1566:
Ancient Records

Some researchers, following leads like the Ezekiel story, have sought UFOs in the early texts of every major civilization. They have found many.

Raymond Drake wrote a series of books based upon his research and uncovered hundreds of possible 'sighting reports'. Each culture described UFOs in relevant terms. To the Romans they were 'burning shields'; to the dwellers of the Indian sub-continent during the mythic age chronicled in the *Mahabaharata*, they were gods who flew in 'vimana' –

deadly lances that spread through the skies.

Of course, some tales may only be legends – but then even legends usually have some basis in fact. Others were undoubtedly genuine records of things beyond the understanding of the great minds of the age. It is only in very recent times that science has unearthed the secrets of the stars and our own world, revealing phenomena like meteors and aurora. A few hundred years ago such things would seem like miracles. Even a rainbow must have once been a UFO, because UFO – quite literally – stands for *Unidentified* Flying Object. Rainbows were that for quite a long time.

In truth, most things to be seen in the sky were UFOs until we came to understand them. Logically, of course, today there must still be things that we have yet to explain. Some of our UFOs will become wonders of nature that are taught in school to the children of the next millenium.

There is also a danger of retrospective hoaxing. With the popularity of the UFO mystery it can be a tease to create an ancient sighting. Supposed records of a spacecraft sailing above baffled monks at a Yorkshire abbey in AD 1290 and a contact by a cabinet-maker on a hill in Buckinghamshire during Victorian times have been exposed as fabrications.

The latter formed the basis of the 1979 book by science writer David Langford, entitled *An Account of a Meeting With Denizens of Another World*. Even today some people cheer the revelation of the modern world's first alien contact (reputedly occurring on 4 October 1871). Sadly, Langford confirms it is nothing more than a clever hoax that he invented.

Nevertheless, there are accounts that can be taken seriously. There was a woodcut etching found by psychologist Carl Jung in the central Zurich library when he researched UFOs towards the end of his life. This relates details of an actual incident at Basel in Switzerland, dated 7 August 1566.

The probability is that this was some form of unusual optical phenomenon associated with the sun; there are a number of similar cases in European archives from the same period. However, we still do not recognize what was seen and to those citizens it was just as much a UFO as many baffling sightings made today.

12 AUGUST 1883:
Photographic Proof

During the nineteenth century astronomers often saw 'meteors' which behaved oddly. They described them in their learned publications but had no UFO mystery in which to slot them. Then one man and his camera snapped the world's first UFO photograph.

It happened at the observatory at Zacatecas, eleven thousand feet up a Mexican mountain. The director, José Bonilla, had been investigating sunspots and was using a camera attached to the telescope to record them. But strange things were going on at the same time. Glowing objects were crossing the face of the sun and he took pictures to prove this was no hallucination.

Bonilla reported in the astronomical press:

I was able to fix their trajectory across the solar disk . . . some appeared round or spherical, but one notes in the photographs that the bodies are not spherical but irregular in form. Before crossing the solar disk these bodies threw out brilliant trains of light but in crossing the sun they seemed to become opaque and dark against its brighter background.

One of the objects he photographed resembled a 'five-pointed star with dark centre'. There was some inevitable speculation that these were birds or luminous insects crossing the path of his telescope. However, Bonilla was convinced that the objects were outside the earth's atmosphere and from measurements of their motion claimed he was able to judge them to be not quite as far out as the moon.

He was the first person to prove he saw a UFO by taking its photograph. He would not be the last.

NOVEMBER 1896:
The Airship Waves

As the nineteenth century drew to a close, Western society dreamed of powered flight. Inventors were experimenting with balloons and dirigibles. The new breed of science-fiction authors were equally excited. Jules Verne published *Robur the Conqueror* in 1892 and showed that air domination in warfare could prove total. Horrific 'air raids' were invented soon from H. G. Wells.

From a mixture of fact and fiction came the airship waves – the first concentrated spate of UFO activity localized in time and space. Waves are now a major part of the UFO evidence, cropping up from time to time all over the world. In 1896 there was still no UFO mystery, so the baffling sightings were seen as the result of real airships.

Although there were earlier isolated examples, the night of 17 November 1896 introduced the story to the people of Sacramento, the state capital of California. Many townsfolk saw 'an electric arc lamp propelled by some mysterious force'. Often it was just a light drifting through the night, but there were daylight sightings across the state as well. Other witnesses swore the light had been attached to an object shaped like a fat cigar – exactly what an airship was expected to resemble. Was a real airship built in secret and flown all over California? The debate raged.

The press reacted much as today. Some treated it with scepticism – a top professor terming the stories a 'freemasonry of liars'. Others saw the rapidly accumulating stories as observations of something strange. A few newspapers simply recognized the potential for a 'good story' and printed yarns about messages from the mysterious inventors, threats to attack Cuba (then in dispute with the USA) and landings of various craft and occupants (almost always eccentric but human).

The original wave in California was replaced by a broader spread of airship sightings throughout the mid-west of America during spring 1897.

Jerome Clark, of CUFOS (the Center for UFO Studies), studied original records and notes that much of the press exaggeration was due to 'frontier humour' – the tall tales of bravado that settlers taming the west would still tell during the 1890s. Several key airship stories were exposed as hoaxes, emerging from this unique free spirit. One example is the spaceman killed by residents of Aurora, Texas. Then there are the celebrated claims of Alexander Hamilton.

Hamilton reported a cow being kidnapped by an airship at Le Roy, Kansas, in April 1897. This has become a 'classic' of the UFO world and, even in 1991, a major book by respected writer John Spencer presents it unchallenged. Unfortunately, it is no such thing.

Hamilton was involved with a town 'liars' club', where members competed to see who could tell the most unbelievable story. Folklore researcher Dr Thomas Bullard has even established that the man himself admitted the hoax in the local press just a few days after it was first published. Yet sincere people were reporting things which they could not identify. Today with our superior aware-ness of the world about us we recognize many of these lights as meteors or the planet Venus. But what we now call UFOs were certainly also flying around amidst the airship waves.

More reports followed in New Zealand and Australia. But it was in Britain where they made the most impact – during 1909 and 1912. Typical of the sightings was that made by P.C. Kettle at Peterborough, on 23 March 1909, where he described a buzzing engine and saw a powerful lamp attached to a dark, oblong body.

By 1909 some real airships were successfully flying and there was much fear of invasion by Germany, who were leaders in airship construction. To ordinary people the possibility that these might be used in war was every bit as real as the threat of nuclear missiles today.

After an airship drifted over the naval dockyards at Sheerness in Kent on 14 October 1912, Winston Churchill (then first lord of the Admiralty) made a parliamentary statement saying the object was definitely *not* British. Count Zeppelin insisted it was not German. History was to later prove both men right. Churchill had become the first politician to admit in public the existence of unexplained objects in the sky. UFOs were now recognized officially – forty years before the term was invented!

25 FEBRUARY 1942:

The Invasion of Los Angeles

Only weeks after the Japanese sneak attack on Pearl Harbor, the western coast of the USA was on war alert. In the early hours of 25 February 1942 these fears seemed vindicated. The city of Los Angeles was blacked out, citizens panicked, anti-aircraft teams were called to arms and for an hour they fired a barrage of shells into the air.

Photographs show searchlights blazing through the night and the flak bursting into empty sky – but there are no enemy aircraft. Certainly none were shot down. Yet three people on the ground were killed accidentally.

On 25 February 1942, UFOs were reported over Los Angeles, California. The sightings were linked to a Japanese invasion that never happened, but real gunfire was aimed at the phantom objects, as shown here.

The official report on the incident termed it a false alert caused by war nerves. Yet witnesses reportedly saw a large dark object that drifted down the coast towards Santa Monica – unfazed by the ferocious anti-aircraft fire.

In 1987 UFO researcher Timothy Good released a document obtained under the Freedom of Information Act in the USA. It had been kept secret for over thirty years. This was a memo to President Roosevelt from his chief-of-staff and written just twenty-four hours after the incident. The report clearly indicated that despite the denials, 'unidentified airplanes, other than American army or navy planes, were probably over Los Angeles'.

Was this a military excuse to hide the tragic chaos, or an admission that real unidentified aerial objects were the cause of a false alarm? Steven Spielberg parodied the event in the film *1941*.

WORLD WAR TWO:
The 'Foo' Fighters

During the final three years of the war, Allied pilots in most theatres of operation had occasional encounters with small balls of light that seemed to chase their aircraft. The assumption was that these were an electrical discharge, like St Elmo's Fire, which can appear on aircraft wing tips. However, these strange balls were free floating and when enough reports came in, the diagnosis had to change.

Were these objects Nazi secret weapons – maybe attempts to scramble radar? If so, they continued to appear with little effect and there does not seem to have been much official interest in them, presumably because of that.

After the war it was discovered that they were neither Nazi nor Japanese weapons, and that the air crew of those nations had seen them too. It now seems clear that these were encounters with the 'ball of light' UFO type that is still frequently seen. In fact, it is not surprising that a wave had resulted.

For the first time in history thousands of aircraft were in the skies at one time, vastly increasing the chances of an aerial close encounter. During a war it was inevitable that sightings of 'secret weapons' resulted because of the assumption that the lights were hostile.

The American pilots gave the mystery the name 'Foo fighter' after a cartoon character called Smokey Stover, then popular in their ranks. His catch phrase was 'where there's *foo* there's fire'.

A typical report is offered by Lieutenant David McFalls of America's 415th night-fighter squadron. At six p.m. on 22 December 1944 he was flying over Alsace-Lorraine on the France/Germany border when he saw:

> . . . *Two very bright lights [that] climbed up towards us from the ground. They levelled off and stayed on the tail of our plane. They were huge, bright orange lights. They stayed there for two minutes. . . Then they turned away from us and the fire seemed to go out.*

Several photographs exist which reputedly show Foo fighters. One of the clearest depicts two of them, right beside a pair of Japanese fighters. It is believed that this photograph dates from around 1942 and was taken in the Pacific.

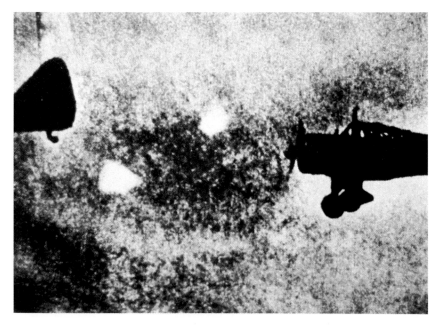

A typical 'Foo-fighter' story from the Second World War illustrated by a photograph to prove the mystery was real. These bright balls of light tailed aircraft of both the Allies and Axis powers. Nobody knew what they were but they appear today to have been classic ball-of-light UFOs.

After the Second World War there were various attempts to build a flying-saucer shaped aircraft. All the projects ended in failure, but there are rumours that the Nazis came very close during the last days of the war. This is an American example from the early 1950s.

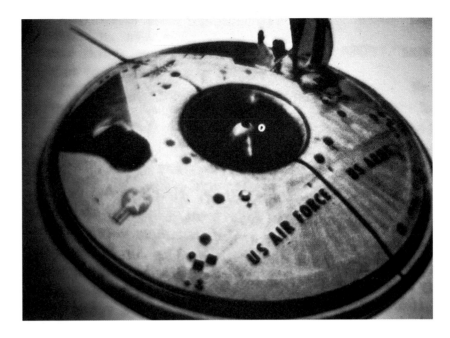

MAY 1946:
The Ghost Rockets

When the Second World War ended there were many rumours about the prowess of German scientists. One of the most popular, for which there is some evidence, is that they were working on a plate-shaped aeroform. This reputedly made its first flight in February 1945, just before Hitler's demise. If successful, it may have changed the outcome of the war. When the Allies invaded, all prototypes and plans were destroyed to stop them falling into enemy hands.

This object was said to closely resemble a real-life 'flying saucer'. Aviation companies and at least one secret US military project, tried to build a 'saucer-shaped' aircraft in the years immediately after the war. Photographs exist of one such device but the experiments were rapidly abandoned when the design proved aero-dynamically unstable.

The Nazis were also working on the world's first intercontinental missile to carry bombs direct to American cities. In the cold war period there was much fear that the Soviet Union might gain such technology.

As a result, it was not surprising that the wave of UFO activity in Sweden, which began a year later, caused considerable worry in Whitehall and Washington. It seemed likely that the Soviet Union was testing captured Nazi rockets for new levels of performance.

Almost a thousand sightings were logged by Swedish defence agencies during 1946 – mostly describing identical things. Research by UFOlogists Anders Liljegren and Klas Svahn uncovered a sighting by a military serviceman at the Oscar Fredricsborg base near Stockholm in daylight on 30 July. The serviceman saw a 'flying object [which had] short wings and no sound at a distance of about two thousand meters. Speed was greater than a jet aircraft'.

The objects roared across the air and fell steeply out of the sky – creating a rocket-like impression. A photograph taken on 9 July shows a teardrop with a flaming tail falling almost vertically downward, but investigators believe that this (like many sightings) was a bright meteor.

Although eighty per cent of all sightings were solved in this way the Swedish military drew back from dismissing the wave. It was never satisfactorily resolved and decades later it still seems puzzling.

In their final report dated 23 December 1946, the commander-in-chief of the Swedish investigation admitted his team had been defeated:

> Despite the extensive effort which has been carried out with all available means, there is no actual proof that a test of rocket projectiles has taken place over Sweden . . . [but] the committee cannot dismiss certain facts as being purely public imagination.

It is believed that some of those 'certain facts' included radar trackings of objects travelling at speeds way beyond those of conventional aircraft and yet slower than meteors. Whatever the ghost rockets were, their cause was once again unidentified. Another wave of UFO activity had occurred without being recognized.

24 JUNE 1947:
Enter the 'Flying Saucers'

With the Second World War now a memory, the American press were keen to find lighter things to discuss. A perfect opportunity arrived on a Tuesday afternoon, 1947, in high summer. This was not the first UFO sighting in this latest wave sweeping the rugged north-western states of Washington and Oregon, but it proved to be the first to achieve instant attention. An expanding mass media included radio and TV stations free from wartime restrictions, so the encounter of private pilot Kenneth Arnold was flashed around the world. The UFO mystery was born.

Arnold was a businessman flying his light plane from Chehalis in Washington across the breathtaking scenery of the Cascade Mountains towards Yakima. A US marine transport plane had been lost and a five-thousand-dollar reward was posted for its recovery. Motivated by this and his responsibilities as a fellow aviator, Arnold made a detour to

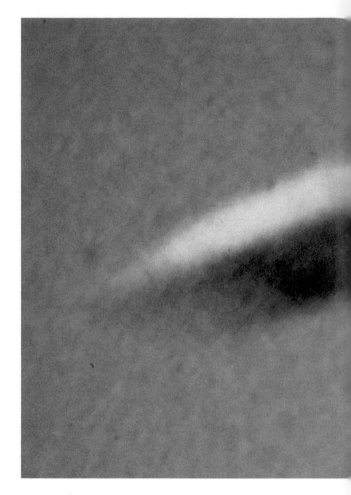

look for it. Instead he was surprised by several brilliant flashes of light on his canopy.

In his privately published report recounting the historic event Arnold tells us what he saw:

> I observed far to my left and to the north, a formation of very bright objects coming from the vicinity of Mount Baker, flying very close to the mountain tops and traveling at tremendous speed . . . I watched as these objects rapidly neared the snow border of Mount Rainier, all the time thinking to myself that I was observing a whole formation of jets. In group count . . . they numbered nine. They were flying diagonally in an echelon formation . . . What startled me most at this point was the fact that I could not find any tails on them.

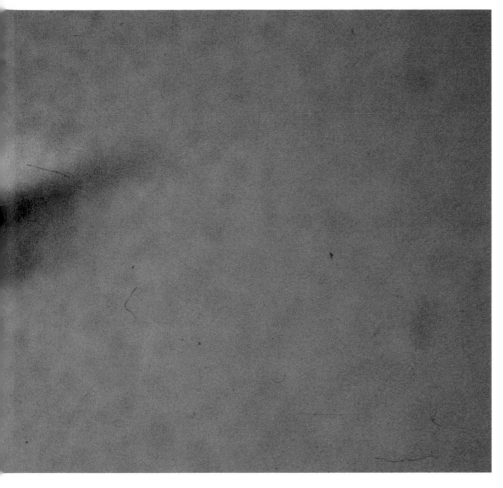

It has become traditional to think of UFOs as saucer shaped, like the object pictured here, although many sightings describe other shapes including balls of light and rocketlike projectiles.

Arnold did a lot of sensible things – using his dashboard clock to judge the time taken for the objects to traverse known distances from peak to peak, and opening his canopy to rule out sun reflections. He eventually concluded that these were some new government device because he had measured a speed far beyond that any aircraft could reach. Of course, this was completely dependent upon his estimate that the objects were over twenty miles away from him at closest approach.

Astronomer and pioneer UFOlogist Dr J. Allen Hynek later established this to be an impossibility. At that distance the objects would have had to be huge in order to be seen – far larger than Arnold reported. More likely they were smaller in size and closer to him, so their speeds became much more like those of ordinary aircraft. It is even possible that they were far smaller and closer than Arnold thought, and were a flock of birds reflecting the strong sunlight to appear unusual. Many similar 'formations' of UFOs reported since 1947 have turned out to be precisely that.

Arnold's drawing of the objects is very birdlike. It shows that they had two well-defined, swept-back wings and no resemblance to colourful artists' impressions of UFOs found in many books about him in later years. These boats assume he described a near-perfect saucer, with a tiny 'bite' cut out – not what Arnold saw. The belief that he did see a saucer stems from a highly significant misunderstanding.

Waves of UFO sightings before 1947 describe balls of light, rocketlike projectiles or airships. None are of the traditional saucer-shaped craft which we associate with the UFO (indeed the name 'flying saucer' implies this shape). Arnold's influential report was a completely different variety. By no stretch of the imagination was it saucer-shaped.

The reason for this discrepancy is explained by Arnold. When he landed at Yakima he told friends what he had seen. By the time he had flown on to Pendelton, Oregon, the media was waiting. He wrote, 'As I put it to newsmen . . . they flew like a saucer would if you skipped it across water.'

He was referring to the (again birdlike) swooping *motion* of these nine objects as they 'bounced' through the air – *not* to their shape. Yet one journalist saw how useful it was to invent a name for the mystery. Arnold's UFOs became 'flying saucers'

and the whole world assumed that he saw objects that *looked* like saucers. People started to report exactly that!

More sightings poured in, delighting the media. One simple story had triggered an avalanche as everyone began to look to the skies with new interest. Editors were keen to keep the pot boiling.

But there was a big difference between this wave and that of 1896. Then everybody 'knew' that the cigar-shaped UFOs were airships built by secret inventors. After government denials, nobody knew what Arnold's 'saucers' could be. They were a mystery and, like all good mysteries, were great fun for everyone to try to solve. As a result, a great debate ensued and the mystery was created.

► A UFO spotted over Denmark on 3 May 1974 represents the type which at that time former USAF consulting scientist Dr. J. Allen Hynek was calling 'The Daylight Disc'. After 1974 such objects were to become increasingly rare, but nobody has yet explained why this should be so.

◄ Images of UFOs have been flashed all over the world by the mass media.

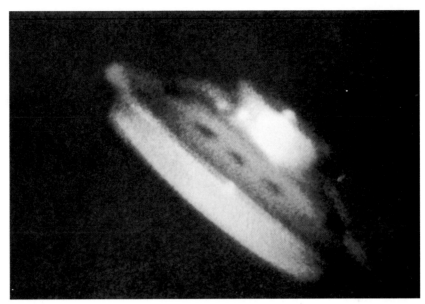

2 JULY 1947:
Crash Go the Saucers

Within days of Arnold's sighting, America went UFO crazy. Some reports were no doubt hoaxes. Others were probably cases of mistaken identity of natural phenomena which people had never really noticed before.

Perhaps mindful of what had occurred recently in Scandinavia, a military enquiry was launched in understandable secrecy. The Americans knew that if advanced craft were flying the skies they were not the product of Uncle Sam and so, potentially, were a threat.

The Soviet Union did not have the resources or technology. Gradually the team of experts and scientists reviewing the rapidly expanding evidence contemplated the awesome thought that craft might be arriving from somewhere *off* the earth altogether.

A report was submitted in early 1949, but the chief-of-staff reputedly sent it back, refusing to take such an astonishing statement to the President. Yet Massachussetts Institute of Technology (MIT) professor George Valley, a senior presidential adviser, said in his section of the report:

If there is an extraterrestrial civilization which can make objects as are reported . . . such a civilization might observe that on earth we now have atomic bombs and are fast developing rockets . . . they would be alarmed. We should, therefore, expect at this time above all to behold such visitations.

This view apparently had influence and – for some – is a symptom of the belief still dominant in UFO circles. Many insist that the American government not only suspected, but actually *knew* from that first week in 1947 that the objects behind the mystery were alien craft. Such an opinion is fuelled by the incident near Roswell, New Mexico, which remains the most hotly debated of all UFO sightings.

A rancher named William Brazel heard an explosion amidst a fierce storm. Next day, 3 July 1947, he found some wreckage strewn over the desert. This was weird – very light, like balsa wood – yet shiny and metallic in appearance. Its composition was pliable but could not be dented with a sledgehammer. Other pieces had strange symbols on them.

Brazel notified the local airbase at Roswell. Intelligence officer Jesse Marcel collected as much debris as he could and ferried it back to the compound. An official press release claimed that the

In the early 1950s speculation was intense that UFOs were alien. A number of photographs surfaced that supposedly depict captured 'little men' from crashed UFOs. This is one from Germany which, as in all known cases, turned out to be a crude hoax – usually a newspaper 'April Fools' stunt.

A P Villa took several spectacular daylight photographs of a UFO which at the time were amongst the most vivid ever recorded. The date was 16 June 1963 and the location near Albuquerque, New Mexico, within a region noted for many extraordinary close encounters.

stories about 'flying discs' were now fact. Wreckage from one had been recovered. It was to be flown to Wright Patterson Air Force Base in Dayton, Ohio for detailed investigation. But a higher authority intervened and a second release was rapidly substituted. Photographers were allowed to take distant shots of metal fabric seemingly from a weather balloon. They were told that this was all that had been recovered – a felled balloon with a radio sounding device, which the men on the Roswell base had simply failed to identify.

Marcel insisted to the end of his life that this was untrue. The material 'was something I had never seen before or since . . . it certainly wasn't anything built by us'. According to legend the real wreckage *did* go to Wright Patterson even as this diversionary 'balloon' wreck was put on show. Some say the Roswell material still exists in Ohio alongside more complete crashed UFO wreckage and bodies of their crew. They are supposedly kept in a secure facility where for years scientists have tried to reproduce their secrets. The science-fiction film *Hangar 18* immortalizes such stories.

Several rumours and tall tales about other UFO

crashes, and very dubious photographs of captured aliens surfaced over the next few years. The Roswell incident was eventually forgotten – until William Moore and Stanton Friedman published their search for eye-witnesses in 1980. They proved that the weather balloon explanation was a hastily concocted cover story.

Since then, the case has been researched by many different groups and several books on the subject appeared in 1991, revealing results of exhaustive interviews with residents of Roswell, relatives of those involved and the dwindling few eye-witnesses still left alive.

That something occurred in the desert near Roswell has been established beyond all reasonable doubt. Yet, given the strategic location of the site, was the craft earthly in origin? The first atom bombs had been tested nearby, only twenty-four months earlier. Roswell housed the world's only atomic bomber squadron. Secret research into rocketry went on here. It is conceivable that New Mexico might have been just the place to attract alien visitors, but it is equally possible that this was where deeply secret experimental craft were tested. If

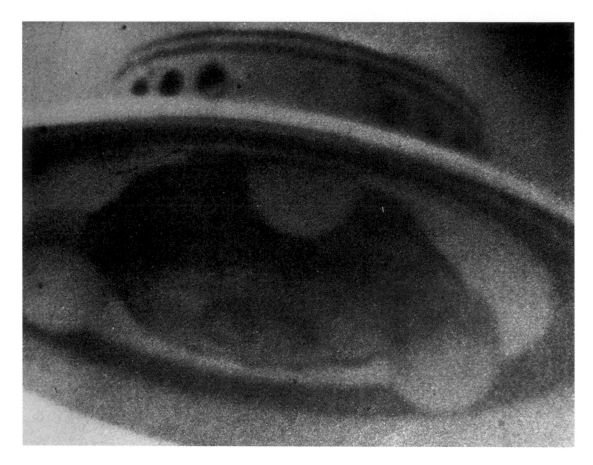

one of those crashed in July 1947, few would have recognized it. Given the recent UFO publicity, a 'flying saucer' story may have seemed the obvious answer.

20 NOVEMBER 1952:
Alien Contact

George Adamski was by all accounts an amiable man in his sixties. He called himself 'professor' and had a great interest in life on other worlds; he ran a café on the slopes of Mount Palomar near the space observatory.

Between 1946 and 1952 he claims to have had several sightings of UFOs – both cigar-shaped and disk-like craft – and photographed many. One day he had an urge to drive into the searing heat of the Californian sun and whilst standing near Desert

Contactee George Adamski took the world by storm in the mid-1950s with tales of trips to the planets. He produced several photographs which allegedly show Venusian spacecraft. Widely rejected by UFO researchers, there have since been some authenticated sightings of very similar UFOs. This Adamski shot was taken at Mount Palomar, California in December 1952.

Center – with some companions well behind – a figure reportedly beckoned across the sands. It turned out to be a man from Venus – humanlike with long blond hair and a suntanned complexion. Communication followed in sign language and images drawn into the ground.

Irish UFO writer, Desmond Leslie, helped compile this story into a book which appeared in 1953 as *Flying Saucers Have Landed*. It became an international bestseller. Adamski produced more photographs and ever more incredible stories through further books, describing trips to see trees and rivers on the moon and visits to the Saturnian high council. Many other so-called contactees came after him claiming friendly alien communication. The UFO field took on an element of religious zeal as conventions sprang up to spread messages of peace and love from alien races with suspicious-sounding science-fiction names.

Although serious UFOlogists saw Adamski and his contemporaries as a threat to their credibility, his tales appealed to the public. Few had a bad word to say. Later he was even asked to meet the Pope!

Adamski's photographs do not convince scientists, but there have been plenty of reliable sightings of near identical craft. These are typical 'sau-

cers' with three ball-like spheres set into the flat base of a bell-shaped dome. Most notable was the experience of teenager Stephen Darbishire on 15 February 1954.

On a hill at Coniston in Cumbria, he was with his younger cousin taking photographs when an 'Adamski' craft reportedly appeared. Stephen took two shots of the object as it climbed skywards but wrongly set his camera. The fuzzy image shows a remarkable close-up of a craft with typical Adamski features. Complex measurements by an aeronautical engineer later allegedly showed that the two craft were identical.

Stephen Darbishire recently told UFO investigator Harry Hudson that prior to the incident he had never read Adamski's story and that he was interviewed by British Intelligence after the sight-

On 4 February 1954, two youths at Coniston in the Lake District, England observed a UFO remarkably like that shown in the Adamski pictures. One unfortunately fuzzy photo was taken by witness Stephen Darbishire. Comparison with Adamski's evidence from two years earlier seems to suggest they are the same object, but the youth claims not to have heard the contactee's story when he took this picture. The now adult witness is a professional man. He confirmed in 1991 that he stands by his story.

MYSTERY OF THE MEN IN BLACK

THE UFO SILENCERS

Introduction by bestselling "Haunted Planet" author JOHN KEEL

◄ A recent book from America shows the lure of the 'Men in Black' legend – sinister people that reputedly began to visit witnesses from about 1952 (when the CIA first took a deep interest in UFOs). Opinion is divided as to whether this is just a myth, or they are government agents. Some say they are part of the UFO mystery itself. Some MIB visits are still reported today.

► UFO encounters do not only involve distant lights in the sky. On 19 August 1952 'Sonny' Desvergers, a scoutmaster, stood beneath a UFO in swampland near West Palm Beach, Florida. Beams of energy shot down and burnt his cap. The US Air Force were baffled, especially when lab tests showed that the roots of the grass beneath where the UFO hovered were singed by radiated heat but the exposed stems were completely untouched.

ing. This team included figures who wore dark glasses. Britain's defence secretary later questioned him.

Official interest in UFO sightings was a novelty in Britain in 1954. A series of mid-air encounters involving RAF jets had shaken Whitehall and many witnesses from 1952 onwards say they were interrogated by secret government investigators. Similar official visitors in the USA – again often wearing dark glasses – became a part of UFO lore during the mid-Fifties, where they are considered to be aliens in disguise.

This legend of the 'men in black' survives and today witnesses still claim to be visited by them. They report being asked odd questions, told not to mention their sighting in public and allege attempts to persuade them that their UFO was really something mundane – such as military aircraft.

2 NOVEMBER 1957:
The UFOs Bare Their Teeth

In October 1957, the world entered the space age when the Soviet Union launched its first sputnik. It came as the American government were trying to wish UFOs into oblivion. The military investigation team were under orders from the CIA to fix the statistics and claim there were hardly any unsolved cases left. Unfortunately, the facts did not support this juggling trick.

A statistical research team at one of the USA's top science centres – the Battelle Memorial Institute had conducted a major survey of the UFO evidence in top secret. American officials hoped it would rid them of the problem. Instead, it really proved UFO reality, showing that the better calibre the witness and the higher quality the evidence, the less likely the sighting was to be explained. So leaders of the US Air Force investigation squad were ordered never to mention the unknown cases! The head, Edward Ruppelt, resigned in dismay and in 1956 produced his own book – *The Report on Unidentified Flying Objects* – the first objective analysis of sightings. This introduced the term UFO to the English language, as a replacement for the now contactee-tainted 'flying saucer'.

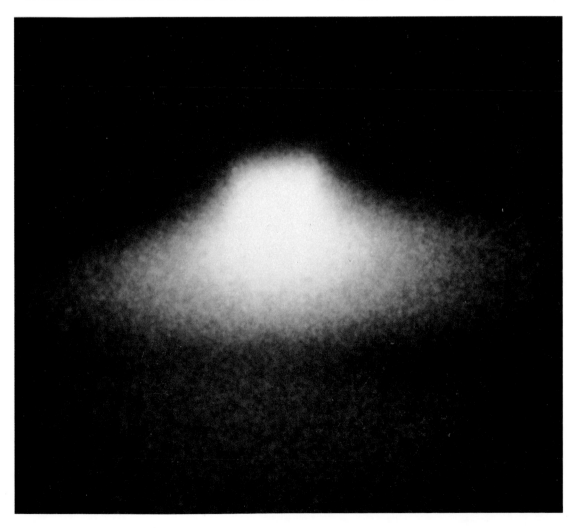

As if in response, the night of 2 November 1957 heralded an astonishing display of power by the UFOs to forever alter their image of being unassuming lights in the sky.

In three hours either side of midnight, up to twenty separate close encounters were reported to police from within a ten-mile radius of the town of Levelland, Texas. Witnesses included drivers of cars, fire fighters and two police patrols, who all described the same thing. Their stories are typified by Pedro Saucido, who saw a brilliant glow emerge from a field:

[it] started towards us, picking up speed. When it got nearer the lights of my truck went out and the motor died. I jumped out and hit the deck as the thing passed directly over the truck with a great sound and rush of wind. It sounded like thunder and my truck rocked from the blast. I felt a lot of heat.

Almost every vehicle involved lost all power – which mysteriously returned when the huge glowing egg had vanished. One frightened witness described how the object was pulsing in rhythm with his car headlights!

No thunderstorm was in the area, but officially this case was passed off as 'ball lightning' – a rare electrical phenomenon. Yet scientists researching this topic do not think ball lightning can appear so many times in different places – nor do they think it can attack cars or drain power as this UFO did.

This demonstration of technological superiority has been repeated many times since 1957, although never on the same scale. In a 1967 case at Sopley, near Bournemouth, a car and diesel-powered truck were approached by a similar object. Both lost their lights but the truck's diesel engine continued to operate. The British Defence Ministry interviewed the three witnesses at length in a local hotel. Next day the road surface at the site was replaced and

The US Air Force employed the Battelle Memorial Institute to carry out a major statistical study. Their hope was that it would prove that UFOs were all poorly reported cases of mistaken identity. In fact, it established that the unsolved cases were puzzles because they had the best-calibre information. The Air Force quickly stopped discussing their unsolved cases!

a nearby telephone booth repainted!

Over five hundred 'vehicle interference' cases have been recorded up to 1991.

24 APRIL 1964:
The UFOs Have Landed

As the Soviet and American space programmes reached their height, the UFOs took to a dramatic new phase of activity. They landed.

A turning point was the sighting made by Lonnie Zamora, an impeccable highway patrol officer and respected member in his local church. He was chasing a speeding car at 5.45 p.m. near Socorro, New Mexico when he heard a roar or explosion which seemed to come from a hut used to store dynamite.

Zamora abandoned the chase and drove to the rocky area where he saw a metallic egg about the size of a car sitting on the ground. Two figures, human in appearance and wearing white coveralls, briefly appeared nearby.

Blue flames like those from a welding torch began to erupt from the base of the object and a frightening noise increased in pitch. Fearing disaster, Officer Zamora ran to shield himself behind his car. As he did so the noise stopped. When he looked back the flames had gone and the object was flying away towards the south-west. It narrowly missed the hut.

Sergeant Chavez had been monitoring Zamora's radio reports. Had he not taken a wrong turn en route to offering assistance, he would have arrived before the UFO left. However, the sergeant was in time to see a shaken Zamora staring at the scrub. A bush was smoking and four holes were impressed into the soil, imprints matching the landing legs on the craft.

An extensive investigation by the US Air Force failed to put a dent in this story. Some later argued that the object might have been a prototype lunar landing module, like those used in the Apollo missions. However, history shows that this solution cannot work. Dr J. Allen Hynek, then the chief scientific consultant with the American team, found this case most impressive.

Just over a year later, at 5.45 a.m. on the morning of 1 July 1965, a farmer at Valensole in France had a remarkably similar experience. There had been mysterious disappearances of his lavender crop when he came upon two small 'boys' examining his plants beside an unusual-looking 'helicopter'. However, on close inspection the 'boys' turned out to be strange beings under four-feet tall with large dome-shaped, bald heads and slanting eyes.

The craft was again a white egg the size of a car standing on legs. The farmer approached the beings with concern and one detached a tube from a belt on its coverall uniform. A beam emerged and the man was instantly paralysed. When he recovered the entities had clambered into the object, which took off with a terrific whistling noise. Years later his lavender crop would still not grow properly at this spot.

During the 1960s the space race captured the imagination of the world. This lure remains, even as re-usable space shuttles are launched from Cape Canaveral, Florida. The prospect of alien contact is at the heart of the fascination of the UFO phenomenon.

3 DECEMBER 1967:
Alien kidnappers

In the wake of such evidence the American government came under pressure in congress. As a result, a scientific team was set up at the University of Colorado in Boulder, near Denver, under the direction of Dr Edward Condon.

Condon had been one of the physicists in the Manhattan Project, building the atom bomb under intense secrecy. From the start of the two-year UFO investigation he made no secret about his lack of faith in the phenomenon.

Nevertheless, many scientists in the team were impressed. Some even left and wrote an alternative report, disillusioned by Condon's attitude. In conclusion, Condon had claimed that UFOs were of no interest to science, but the thousand-page study proved the opposite. Over one-third of the selected cases were left unexplained. Scientists working on radar sightings, landings and photographic evidence

During the NASA flights, strange objects were sometimes reported by astronauts. Most of the photographs that were taken have simple explanations. This November 1966 photograph from the *Gemini 12* mission is thought likely to be debris floating in space, reflecting strong sunlight.

UFOs were often photographed during space missions in the 1960's; although most turned out to have conventional explanations. A few remain unidentified. Here some odd lights are seen near the moon's surface.

concluded again and again that the best answer to an incident was a *real* UFO. It is said that Condon's report persuaded many that UFOs were an unresolved phenomenon – despite his own conclusions.

However, the American government were delighted with this negative viewpoint and in 1969 responded by closing the US Air Force investigation team set up after the 1947 sightings. However, recently released documents show that they insisted that UFO reports should still be examined at official levels!

Another twist to the UFO story had begun when an American couple had seen a UFO in New Hampshire in September 1961. There was a period of 'missing time', which they could not remember. During treatment for anxiety and bad dreams, a psychiatrist 'regressed' them under hypnosis. They relived the experience and a frightening account emerged in which they were 'kidnapped' aboard the UFO and probed by weird beings. Although considered a 'dream' by the doctor, a book by John Fuller was published in 1965 as *The Interrupted*

Journey, and later became a movie – *The UFO Incident*.

Condon's team furthered such research during their study. An incident happened in December 1967 to police officer Herb Schirmer in Ashland, Nebraska. He had encountered an egg-shaped object with tripod legs hovering near electricity pylons when he lost a period of some twenty minutes from his recollection. Hypnosis was carried out by psychologist Dr Leo Sprinkle, now a leader in the study of 'abductions' by aliens. Under hypnosis Schirmer stated that he was forcefully taken aboard the UFO by beings engaged in 'breeding' experiments on humans. His mind was implanted with a 'cover story', where he simply saw the UFO from afar. Sprinkle was convinced Schirmer 'believed in the reality of the events . . .'. Indeed, the officer passed a lie-detector test. Officially, the London committee merely wrote the case off as 'unproven'. Since then these cases have spread around the world. Hundreds claim abduction by aliens carrying out genetic experiments.

19 SEPTEMBER 1976:
Earth Versus the UFOs

When the US Air Force project shut down, Dr J. Allen Hynek formed the Center for UFO Studies. New waves of sightings continued globally and in spite of Condon the subject was reviewed at the American Association for the Advancement of Science (AAAS). In 1978 debate reached the United Nations; initiated by the Premier of Grenada. He became so engrossed he was deposed!

A significant new case set the American defence agencies into a frenzy. Secret documents were later released, but at the time the public knew little of what took place in the skies over Iran.

The Air Force received reports of a big white light in the sky soon after midnight on 19 September 1976. Believing it to be a star they did nothing until a deputy commander saw the object himself from his command post. A Phantom jet was scrambled by Shahrokhi base. At 1.30 a.m. the aircraft closed

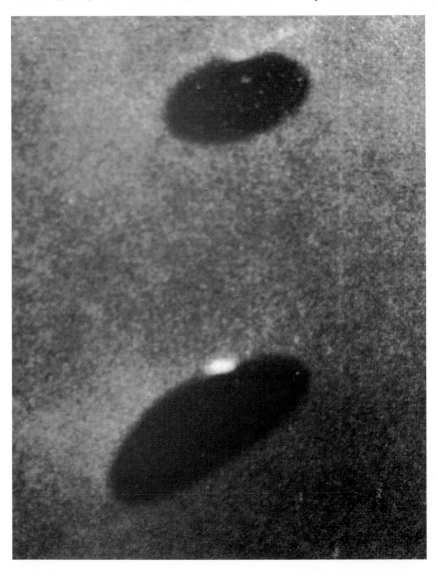

In March 1967 a major UFO sighting took place near Yungay in Peru. This is one of the pictures taken of the event.

30

The UFO mystery has taken on an international appeal. There is scarcely a language that does not have a term for it, although UFO itself is being adopted by many tongues. Popular UFO books often appear far away from their original home – here is a Japanese edition of a story about a UFO landing near a NATO air base in Suffolk, England that occurred in December 1980.

宇宙人との「第４の遭遇」！

ベストセラー『ＭＩＢの謀略』の
矢追純一 訳 の話題作！

世界で初めて公式機関が公文書で宇宙人の飛来を確認！1980年12月27〜30日に英国駐留米空軍将兵らが体験した驚くべき事実とは──

話題の書「第４の遭遇」を改題！緊急出版！

ベストセラー『ＭＩＢの謀略』の矢追純一の話題作

三一書房

in to the north of Tehran, but lost all radio and instrumentation. Forced to break away and turn back, all power immediately returned. The American defence agency said in their report that this suggested a strategy – returning power only when the jet was no longer a threat to the UFO.

A second Phantom was launched and at twenty-five miles from the dazzling UFO it established a radar lock-on. The UFO streaked away but the jet gave pursuit.

An amazing episode followed. The UFO 'launched' a projectile towards the Phantom. Convinced he was about to be attacked, the pilot reacted instinctively to fire a guided missile at the target. As he did so he also lost all power and communication, exactly like his colleague. The missile would not fire. An immediate course change and dive was set into motion to evade the 'projectile'. As if satisfied that its warning had been heeded this then made a sudden U-turn and sailed back into its parent craft.

Moments later a second object ejected and fell vertically downwards, landing softly with a brilliant glow on a dry lake bed in this remote area. Next day the Phantom's crew were taken to this spot. Nothing was found. But at the time it had landed the glow was so intense that the pilot had to circle before he could return to Shahrokhi because his eyes were not adjusted to the dark.

Was this a demonstration of futile earth technology? Four years later at a briefing session inside the British parliament I learnt that UFO investigation was thought essential because nobody understood what went on. The cover-up in force was one of ignorance – not of guilty secrets.

In 1985, as President Reagan and Mikhail Gorbachev met to initiate historic cuts in nuclear weapons, Reagan said that it would be easier if 'suddenly there was a threat to this world from another species from another planet . . .'. Then we would have to stand together. Confrontations between UFOs and aircraft have since become more frequent. Was Reagan hinting at a truth behind these contacts? Did he have UFOs in mind?

For the 1990s the UFO mystery has entered a new phase. Mysterious swirled circles are appearing in great profusion in crop fields around the world. What causes them? Are they an alien message about looming ecological disasters as some propose? This is a typical single circle that appeared in Lancashire, England during August 1990. Most circles are as simple as this.

26 DECEMBER 1980:
An Alien Alliance?

As democracy swept through the world during the 1980s, freedom-of-information laws were passed in most countries and secret files about UFOs in America and Australia became public. Even the Soviet Union launched an enquiry into UFOs in 1985, headed by a former cosmonaut. By 1989 its news agency TASS was endorsing a UFO landing at Voronezh to an astonished world.

Meanwhile, UFO writers were making increasingly dramatic claims. Whitley Strieber's story of his own abduction, *Communion*, became the most widely read UFO book of all time, selling millions around the world. In 1989 it became *Communion: The Movie*, attempting to portray the psychological

terror of experiencing the unknown in frighteningly real surroundings.

Claims about the cover-up by government defence agencies reached new heights. Amidst the documents released under the new laws came others, far more contentious. These told a hidden story of official UFO studies – alleging that the aliens had struck a deal with the American government, giving free rein to their activities and abductions in exchange for alien technology. This gave the Americans huge advantages in air and space. By 1989 it was reputed that alien-built, American-piloted UFOs were flown from a base beneath the Nevada desert. Such tales were widely discredited, even amongst UFOlogists, but the 1991 book, *Alien Liaisons*, by Timothy Good, followed his huge 1987 success, *Above Top Secret*, to create believers out of a surprising number.

One case which seemed to support this occurred on the night after Christmas in 1980 in a Suffolk

pine forest. American airmen from the twin NATO bases of Bentwaters and Woodbridge went out in response to reports of a UFO and observed an object in a clearing which apparently had smashed through trees. One security police sergeant later described what he saw:

It was lit up like a Christmas tree with white and a blue bank of lights. It moved slowly at first, but then it could move so fast and it turned at right angles in an impossible way. I do not know any technology, certainly not in 1980, probably not even now, that could do the things this did. It was just like magic.

The UFO was chased through trees by trained airmen and left holes in the ground, excess radiation and other damage. The next day it returned and was surrounded by the US Air Force, who may have been expecting its arrival, according to some

reports. After it was gone, governments hid the truth, but far too many people had seen something, including civilians in the surrounding villages.

When stories leaked out, the British and American governments were silent – until in 1983 a controlled leak provoked a major furore and questions in parliament. Yet still the full truth of that night was not released.

After years accumulating evidence, I have built up an amazing picture of one of the best documented close encounters ever. There simply must have been the most intense investigation into the matter, yet senior politicians all denied this. Key figures in the House of Commons and the House of Lords were adamant in the face of pressure mounted by UFOlogists and MPs. Even the former chief-of-staff at the Ministry of Defence said something was being hidden.

The landings in Rendlesham Forest triggered far more official reaction than any other case in UFO history, a sure sign that something dramatic took place. One intriguing comment made in January 1990 by the Ministry of Defence in London came in response to a letter from a UFOlogist, asking why there was no investigation. Owen Hartop's reply stated, '. . . the Ministry of Defence was content that the Rendlesham incident was of no defence significance because whatever was witnessed was not apparently hostile.'

But how did they know it was not hostile – unless they knew exactly what it was and were happy to allow its activities to continue?

SUMMER 1991:
Symbols From The Skies

In the same year that the landings took place in Rendlesham Forest, farmers in southern England began to notice strange marks in their fields.

These were swirled circles laid down with beautiful precision. Immediately the suspicion was that UFOs were creating them whilst landing or departing. As more appeared each summer but no UFOs were seen, this theory soon became discredited.

Yet to many it seemed that some intelligence must be responsible for the images. The number of patterns increased in number. They started to appear in other parts of the country and eventually the world, and in ever more complex shapes.

Scientists attempted to show that the circles were the result of rotating air and electrical charges swirling about. Impressive evidence was published. But the artistic designs seemed too much like a message for most believers.

As the debate heated up, so did the publicity. The shapes left in fields became so fantastic that no theory of electrified air appeared likely. By 1991 hundreds of patterns were forming in over thirty countries every summer and the designs were intricate and imaginative – featuring bars, spurs, rings and pictorial imagery. Coincident with this huge rise in crop circle numbers, UFO sightings had fallen to record low levels after Steven Spielberg's 1978 UFO film fable *Close Encounters of the Third Kind*. Had aliens found a new way to try to reach humanity – doodling in crop fields?

Of course, there was a heavy influence from tricksters. People excited by the publicity – and the £10,000 rewards set up in 1990 – engaged in artistic vandalism. The question was: could this explain the entire rise in circle totals? Was there a natural phenomenon forming a few simple patterns and massive hoaxing creating the rest? Or had the scientists got it wrong, as they so often had when dealing with UFOs? Was this really a graphic and unmistakable message to the world about the dangers of ecological disaster?

The circles had become the next great phase of the UFO story. Whilst sightings began to rise again, the circles were dominant. There had been another unexpected twist leaving millions baffled. Was that the point? Was the UFO mystery showing again that it was an intelligence test? Mankind had to solve a puzzle, make the right response and then the phenomenon would change tactics and create a new phase of activity to confound us.

This appropriately brings us full circle to where the UFO story first began and where it has left us all along. What is the meaning of the game? Are alien intelligences seeking to communicate in a way that the world can comprehend? Or are they treating us like rats in a maze in some scientific laboratory? Either way, if we do solve the *final* riddle, what then?

As with UFOs, the media have become attracted by the circles. Here a TV crew for Granada Television in the UK are about to film a news item about a ring that formed overnight in a field in Cheshire in July 1990. Although this ring's origin seems doubtful after investigation, a spoof involving an actor dressed as an alien is about to be staged for the camera – showing how crop circles and UFOs are naturally linked together by many people.

2 IDENTIFIED FLYING OBJECTS (IFOs)

IN MARCH 1966 Joan Oldfield and husband Tom took a flight from Manchester to Southampton aboard a British United Airways Elizabethan aircraft. They planned to see a relative sail for a new life in Australia. As their aircraft climbed into the breakfast sun above north Staffordshire, Mrs Oldfield became aware of an object through the aircraft window. It seemed to be following them. Using the cine-camera brought to film the family departure she pointed the lens towards the clear sky and pressed the button. Shortly afterwards the aircraft banked and the UFO disappeared. But not before they had filmed it – a strange dark cigar with fins which had seemingly altered into an egg-like oval before fading away.

To their delight the film developed, and over ten seconds showed exactly what had been witnessed. This was one of those rare glimpses of a UFO close up – captured for posterity on film.

In 1966 most UFO investigators were naïve. They did not presume a sighting would have an ordinary explanation – especially not if it had been filmed in this way. The case was considered unidentified by most enthusiasts. It had become prime evidence. However, just as in nine out of every ten cases, this proved to be no such thing.

The Oldfields saw an *IFO* – Identified Flying Object. Only careful reconstruction by a BBC film crew resolved the mystery. They flew the route in the same seat on the same aircraft and – sure enough – the UFO reappeared. It turned out to be an unexpected optical illusion created by the double layers in the aircraft window, the angle of light and other factors. The shape-changing UFO was the Elizabethan's own tail fin.

Today's UFO researchers are thankfully more cautious. They are trained to grasp the significance of IFO cases.

A still which shows the object that was filmed by the Oldfields from an aircraft flying above Staffordshire, England in 1966. The explanation for this particular IFO was only found after detailed reconstruction. Most UFO investigations do not have the resources or the luck that this one had, but must still endeavour to find a solution wherever possible.

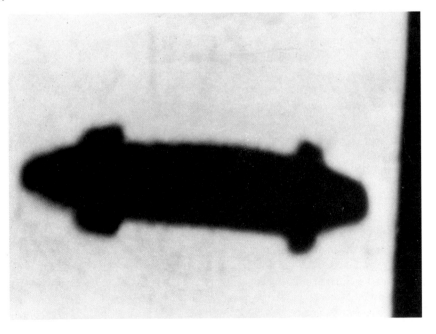

Serious investigation groups and government figures – from the US Air Force projects between 1947 and 1969 and data from the British Ministry of Defence or the Royal Australian Air Force – *all* closely agree. No more than a few per cent of the reported UFO sightings (perhaps as high as eight per cent or as low as three per cent) are describing something truly unexplained. The vast majority are cases of mistaken identity for a huge range of phenomena. Sometimes these have simple solutions. Other times you need clever detective work and access to resources that UFO groups just do not have (as was needed to recreate the Oldfield's flight). Occasionally, finding the explanation requires considerable foresight or the application of lateral thinking.

For example, a glowing UFO which terrified fishermen near woodlands in the British Midlands turned out to be an owl that had eaten decaying fungi and was flying about, quite literally glowing in the dark! In another case, a small fuzzy alien traversing a Yorkshire shopping complex turned out to be an escaped circus dog. It was walking on its hind legs and had run through a pond which had left its hair all matted.

Faced with possibilities like this, nothing can be ruled out. UFOlogists have to accept that chances are very high that any particular UFO sightings will ultimately have an explanation. Indeed, many find this seemingly negative factor the source of much fascination. Investigating sighting reports with no financial backing and only rare prospects of stumbling onto an important piece of evidence might be a thankless task. The privately funded UFO groups such as BUFORA (British UFO Research Association) and CUFOS (the Center for UFO Studies) in America attract those who love puzzle-solving and enjoy the chance to emulate Miss Marples or Sherlock Holmes.

But this high level of IFOs within the UFO evidence does not consign the mystery to the trash can. Even if only three in every hundred sightings are genuine, the numbers mount up when you bear in mind how many millions of sightings have already occurred down the years and all over the world.

The lowest estimate for the true number of unexplained reports is around 200,000. Surveys and polls show that far more sightings have occurred that were simply never reported by the witnesses, out of embarrassment or not knowing who to tell. In truth, well over a million people must have seen a real UFO. You could very well be the next!

How to Spot a UFO

If you are aiming to use this book to try to become a UFO witness – or if you have seen something already and you want to decide for youself whether it was a UFO or an IFO – this section is designed to assist. It is impossible to cover every IFO, because almost two hundred different things have been mistaken for a UFO at some time or another. But the next few pages will help you to rule out many of the simpler options. Both descriptions and, where possible, photographs have been used to act as your guide.

First Steps

If you have seen something strange in the sky, take a piece of paper and attempt to sketch its appearance. Don't worry if you cannot draw. An impression of what was witnessed is all you need. The sooner you can do this after a sighting the better. Memory has a way of distorting images.

Underneath the drawing, write all the words from the following lists which best match what you saw. It does not matter if more than one from any particular list is recorded – but write down at least one from each.

☐ SHAPE Light only
Ball or oval
Had a tail
Odd shape (e.g., triangle)
Structured craft, metallic form

☐ SIZE Starlike point
Small ball
Similar to moon or sun
Larger than the above
Huge

Another photograph taken from outer space which has taxed the analysts. Is this a window bolt reflection or evidence of astronauts boldly going where no man has gone before – in the absence of toilet facilities?

You should now have a piece of paper with a sketch and five or more short statements about what the object looked like or how it behaved. Compare this information with the descriptions of the most common types of IFO in the pages that follow. You should get a good impression of whether you have really seen something unusual or have been fooled by one of the many strange things that can be seen by anyone who is observant.

Don't feel embarrassed if it seems you were mistaken. This has nothing to do with your intelligence or abilities. Witnesses to IFOs have included top scientists, airline pilots and astronauts. Even American President Jimmy Carter once saw an IFO and reported it as a UFO. At times, the atmosphere can create visual distor-tions; something can appear in an unusual way – or a rare phenomenon might occur which you were just lucky enough to see.

All things witnessed are *unidentified* at first. Learning what is up there to be misperceived is part of the excitement. It is very unlikely that the first object you spot will be a real UFO . . . but who knows? Good hunting!

IFOs in Space

In outer space there is no atmosphere to cause distortions, but astronauts have still seen UFOs. Some have been photographed. Often they are the result of the unfiltered sunlight shining off window bolts on the capsule, or debris drifting in orbit close

---

☐ COLOUR White
Blue or greenish
Yellow
Red or orange
Had flashing lights

☐ SPEED Did not move
Very slow, drifting motion
Like aircraft crossing sky
Like speeding car
Very fast – like a rocket

☐ DURATION Couple of seconds or less
Half a minute or just under
Two or three minutes
Several minutes (e.g., ten or twenty)
Over half an hour

to the rocket. There are even reliable cases where mission captains – in the spirit of *Star Trek* – have 'boldly gone where no man has gone before'. Waste matter can create UFOs.

However, we are more concerned with phenomena in space that can be seen from the earth. Here are some of the most common astronomical IFOs that you might encounter. At the end of each section are the key phrases to look for on your list that suggest this particular IFO may be what you saw.

Stars and planets

There are trillions of stars in the universe and some are very bright objects in the sky, despite their enormous distance from earth. There are also several planets in our solar system which can be seen as bright starlike lights. The only ones that are ever likely to provoke UFO sightings are Venus, Mars and Jupiter – especially Venus and Jupiter. Venus is not infrequently brighter than any star when at closest range, and is often prominent just after sunset or just before sunrise.

Both stars and planets will stay in one part of the sky and can take hours to rise and set (unless unseen thin, high cloud covers them). To all intents and purposes they appear *not* to move. But as planets are relatively close and rotate around the sun, they seem to shift position a little from night to night. Stars only do so in any noticeable way over many weeks, as the earth's motion seems to take them around the sun. Even so, if you see a UFO that you feel might be a planet such as Venus, look at the same part of the sky at the same time during the next clear night. Chances are it will be there again. This is the easiest way to confirm a UFO as a star or planet. Real UFOs almost never return to the scene of the crime.

Venus can be so bright, especially in pre-dawn winter mornings when the air is full of ice particles, that it can look far too brilliant to be a planet. Through window glass or binoculars it sometimes seems to develop a shape, because it becomes slightly out of focus in this way.

Another problem is autokinesis, which is a form of apparently automatic motion of a light source, usually in zig-zags or sharp jerky movements around a fixed point. The above photograph of a

UFO, which was in reality the planet Venus when particularly bright, shows this effect. As you can see, the background houses are also blurred, because in truth the light remained still but its apparent movement was caused by the camera shaking slightly when the shutter was pressed. The eyeball moves in a similar way to create autokinesis. The star or planet seems to jerk but it is really your eyes that do so.

⬚ CLUES *shape* (light); *size* (starlike point); *colour* (white or blue); *speed* (did not move – maybe jerked about); *duration* (usually many minutes)

The Moon

Surprisingly enough, the moon has produced quite a few UFO sightings. Of course, we are all familiar with our satellite planet . . . but it can play tricks. When near the horizon, it looks much bigger than when it's high in the sky. In fact, it is actually slightly smaller, but a very powerful optical illusion creates this opposite impression. When in this position mist or cloud near ground level may be present, but in the dark we cannot see this. Mist can distort the image of the moon to make it look like an oddly shaped wedge or oval of deep orange colour.

There are even several examples of witnesses who saw the moon distorted in this way with something silhouetted in front – such as a telegraph pole. As a result they thought they had seen a UFO and an alien figure inside. If you are tempted to smile and think this can never happen to you, next time you see the moon near the horizon try to convince yourself it really is no bigger than when it is high in the sky. You now know this to be true, but you will not be able to stop your eyes deceiving you.

⬚ CLUES: *shape* (ball or oval, perhaps odd shape); *size* (small ball, moonlike or larger); *colour* (red, orange or yellow); *speed* (did not move or slow drifting); *duration* (from couple of minutes, often over half an hour)

Meteors

Perhaps the most common IFOs are meteors. These occur when debris from space enters the atmosphere and burns up with friction as it hits the

A UFO photograph which is in fact the planet Venus. The squiggly image is due to the camera shaking, but shows the autokinesis effect on the human eye. ▶

▼ A bright fireball meteor enters the earth's atmosphere and burns up by friction as an incandescent glow.

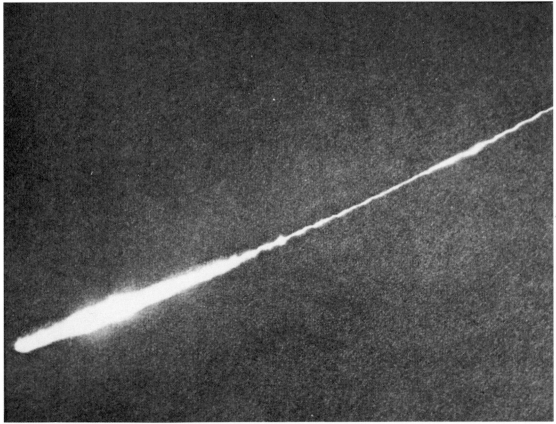

wall of air and is accordingly slowed down. Particles varying in size from microscopic bits to huge rocks (parts of which can reach the earth's surface, as meteorites) lead to a variety of colours, brightnesses and durations. But most meteors are very feeble flickers of light that only briefly illuminate the sky. Thousands of these can be seen from any point on earth each year – up to one hundred an hour during predictable 'meteor showers', on certain nights when the earth's orbit takes it through a field of debris floating in space.

The much rarer spectacular events can last some seconds, be brighter than Venus, and (as with many of the less brighter ones) have a tail. Most locations would probably experience at least one such event per year, if you happened to be looking at the right part of the sky during the few seconds of visibility.

Very bright meteors (sometimes called fireballs)

can often display vivid colours according to the composition of the elements in the debris that is entering the atmosphere.

⊡ CLUES: *shape* (ball or oval, maybe had a tail); *size* (small ball or larger if tailed); *colour* (usually white, can be blue, red, orange, yellow or green); *speed* (at least speeding car, usually rocket-like); *duration* (seconds only)

Space junk

What goes up must come down, they say. That's certainly true of all the satellites and rockets we have sent into orbit. And many of the tens of thousands of bits of derelict junk have gradually wound their way down closer and closer towards the atmosphere where they will eventually become artificial fireball meteors, and plunge to a spectacular

A UFO photograph from Switzerland whose origin is uncertain. But some suspect it shows space junk re-entering the atmosphere and burning up. Certainly this is what a trail of debris from a re-entering satellite can look like.

fiery death. Because they are formed of heavy metal fragments they are slowed more than things like ice and dust, and also take a long time to be consumed in a firework display of multiple colours.

Space junk re-entries can sometimes be predicted. Predictions are necessary because of the chance that debris will reach the earth and create damage on impact. Major re-entry predictions are occasionally reported in advance by the press or on TV as areas at risk can be forewarned. Unfortunately, these areas involve many thousands of square miles and better precision is only possible at the very last minute. Other junk can re-enter with little warning or none at all. An example was a booster rocket from a Soviet satellite whose flaming re-entry on the evening of 31 December 1978 drew fire brigades and police all over Britain and northern Europe to investigate phantom 'air crashes' witnessed by party goers. It also triggered thousands of UFO sighting reports.

Although quite similar in appearance to the brightest fireball meteors, many space junk re-entries are even more dramatic. They move more slowly and so can be visible for longer. Often the rocket breaks into a train of molten pieces and so a chain of trailing fireballs or blobs of light might cross the sky in series. Colours may be vivid.

Danger of being struck is remote but space junk re-entry is among the most amazing IFO sights that can be witnessed by the lucky few.

⊡ CLUES: *shape* (ball, oval or odd shape, usually had a tail); *size* (usually size of the moon at least); *colour* (usually white, blue or red); *speed* (like speeding car in sky or slower); *duration* (two or three minutes)

A spectacular UFO picture taken by Roy Sandbach over Stockport, Cheshire. In fact, it really shows the effects of a misty atmosphere. The moon is visible top left, shining through mist. The lights in the sky lower right are actually a hotel on a hillside obscured by the mist. UFOs are not always what they seem!

IFOs in the Atmosphere

The atmosphere is like a deep sea of gases. We are all at the bottom looking up – and strange effects can result from this.

In northern latitudes, aurora can create dramatic curtains of light as charged particles give off their glows. Such phenomena seem to have become more common and have appeared further south in recent years.

Also, mirages are not confined to the desert. Most people will have seen what looks like a pool of water on the road ahead on a hot day. This is a mirage of the sky. The light rays are bent so that to us they appear on the road surface. It is the same effect as when you put a pencil in a glass of water – it seems to bend through an optical effect.

Very occasionally, differences in heat between layers of air can create what is called a 'temperature

Typical lenticular cloud formations which can be surprisingly like UFOs.

inversion'. This is, in effect, a mirage waiting to happen. If a ground light, star or aircraft drifts through the line of sight of this patch of sky, its shape will distort and it may seem to jump suddenly as the light rays bend. It will jump back when it passes out of the inversion layer. Anything that seems normal at first – then becomes abnormal for a short time, before returning back to normality – might be the result of such an inversion layer. But the effect is not common.

Clouds

As with the moon it seems surprising that clouds can provoke UFO sightings. But this happens. Indeed, the UFO on the cover of this book is thought by some to be a particularly unusual cloud seen over New Mexico.

Certain clouds – especially those which form near mountains – can take on a lozenge shape that resembles the cigar-like UFO. Called lenticular clouds they can also pile on top of each other and seem to be domed craft. They may move only very slowly – being stalled by the air systems that collide near hills.

There are also noctilucent clouds, which have a composition that reflects light: e.g., from street lamps below. In an otherwise dark sky one of these drifting across the night can look very much like a silent UFO. Another possibility is a chemical cloud released from a factory or reactor plant, which might also give off light in some circumstances.

⊡ CLUES: *shape* (ball or oval, odd shape); *size* (at least similar to moon); *colour* (white, possibly yellow or red, if reflecting lights); *speed* (very slow); *duration* (probably two or three minutes, at least, often much longer)

Sundogs

The sun can create odd effects if its rays shine off ice particles in the air, or reflect through very thin, almost invisibly translucent clouds. As a result,

◄ The photographer was trying to take a picture of an overflying aircraft but accidentally framed a disc-like UFO at the same time. He did *not* see this when pressing the shutter, because it was a bird that flew past unnoticed. It has been frozen in flight as a UFO by the fast shutter speed.

► Peter Warrington bravely stood near the end of the runway at a major airport (with permission) to take this shot of an aircraft with landing lights on, heading straight towards him. From a distance these can readily create the illusion of a UFO.

bright patches of light can appear – as either rings around the sun, which may be dull enough to look like a UFO, or as multiple images.

These effects are usually short-lived and tend to occur nearer sunset.

⊡ CLUES: *shape* (ball or oval); *size* (similar to moon or sun); *colour* (yellow); *speed* (does not move); *duration* (few minutes maximum)

Birds

Birds are such a common sight that we may again not expect them to generate IFOs, but they do in two particular ways.

Firstly, when flying very high in the sky in groups on a very sunny day they can reflect so strongly and seem to move so slowly (because of their great distance) that they look like silvery discs moving in formation. At least one famous film of UFOs, given

intensive scrutiny by scientists, is considered to be a high-flying group of gulls wheeling about. It was so far away that the birds' true origins were disguised to the witness.

A similar effect can occur at night if a flock of birds reflects sheet lightning from down below. Some birds have very reflective underbellies and at certain times of the year (especially late summer, autumn, or early winter, when gathering into flocks) they can give a strange illusion of ghostly forms. Reports of UFO formations – in 'V' or 'echelon' – nearly always have their origins in bird sightings. Real UFOs rarely come in packs.

The other way in which birds generate UFO sightings is when they turn up in photographs. Almost always they were not seen by the camera operator when the picture was taken and the photograph – of something else entirely – captures them in shot accidentally. When the film is developed what can look like an impressive daylight UFO – perhaps a domed disc – magically appears. In fact, the high-speed shutter has frozen the bird mid-flight, with its wings at an angle which produces an illusion.

Many daylight photographs of alleged UFO mysteries eventually turn out to have this solution.

⊡ CLUES: *shape* (ball or oval – possibly in formation); *size* (moon or sun); *colour* (white, possibly yellow or red); *speed* (very slow, drifting); *duration* (two or three minutes)

Technological IFOs

As technology improves, so the number of strange objects in the atmosphere created by it increases. There is always the possibility that UFOs, even if undoubtedly the result of metallic craft, might be built by human hands.

When the US Air Force developed stealth aircraft (to avoid radar detection) it is almost certain they were tested for years around air bases for at the time there were numerous reports of UFOs in the vicinity. New generation aircraft may still be provoking UFO reports when under secret tests today.

There are other types of technology – such as RPVs. These 'Remotely Piloted Vehicles' – or drones – are small craft, like super-sophisticated model aircraft, which can be sent into enemy territory without endangering the lives of pilots. Britain is at the forefront of such design and these craft have often been used in Northern Ireland.

Always beware this possibility if a sighting is near to a military establishment.

Aircraft

With greater concern for the environment, more and more aircraft are appearing with 'quiet' engines that may give off no more than a soft whirr or humming noise. They may seem even quieter if the wind is carrying the sound away from you. An aircraft that looks very close might still seem almost silent.

Strong sunlight can reflect from polished metal bodies when at critical angles (especially around sunrise and sunset). As a result, a cigar-like or egg-shaped object without any trace of wings might be observed.

However, it is at night when aircraft are most likely to be misperceived. Standard navigation light-

A UFO photograph taken in Canada in 1973. Its origin is not known but it resembles well enough the effect one can see when a high-flying aircraft with flashing navigation lights passes over. Even if in this case the answer is something else, the picture shows what to expect. The sequence would be the result of the camera shutter being left open for a few seconds.

ing (white, red and green – both steady and flashing beacons) are commonly reported on UFOs. Scientists argue that UFOs are unlikely to carry navigation lights; although some UFO researchers speculate they do so to simulate aircraft. They can then fly about undetected. Nevertheless, if you see white, red and green lights it is most probable that you are watching some kind of aircraft. Many piercing strobe lights can look blue – so beware of that possibility as well.

When coming in to land, aircraft also switch on powerful searchlight beams at the front. If you happen to be facing an aircraft head-on and it switches to such a beam many miles from touchdown (not unlikely – particularly late at night) it could be many minutes before it gets close enough for you to hear it, or for it to seem to move. If it turns in flight away from your line of sight before that point, you may observe a brilliant ball of light in one position, out of which flashing lights later emerge (when the aircraft gets closer) but which simply go out or fade into a series of smaller lights (when it turns away from you). So are UFOs born.

So many surprising combinations of lights are possible that you should always suspect an aircraft if your sighting occurs anywhere near an airport or on one of the flightpaths that ferry aircraft towards airports. There have been many sightings of

strange UFOs passing over the M6 motorway in north Cheshire, for example. Those passing through or unfamiliar with the area have no idea that aircraft on approach to one of Europe's busiest airports (Manchester) cross the road here.

At night they look very puzzling from oblique angles and the sound can be drowned out by the traffic or the moving vehicle in which you are present. At the other extreme, aircraft can enter final approach to the same airport miles away over the Derbyshire peaks. Because you may be on a road already at some height, well above sea level, the aircraft can seem amazingly low, despite being a great distance from an airport. At night, many witnesses fail to make this connection.

However, even experienced witnesses who do live in the area can be fooled. Two police officers in Cheadle Hulme, Cheshire (where aircraft pass over every couple of minutes at just a few hundred feet in height) were foxed by an unusual triangle display of lighting on a British Airways Tristar jet. It headed towards them from some distance away with engines throttled back so as not to disturb the slumbering populace and was reported as a UFO.

There are even reliable reports of cargo aircraft crew switching off all cabin lights, except a beam that shines on to the tailfin and illuminates the airline logo. In the early hours of the morning with no

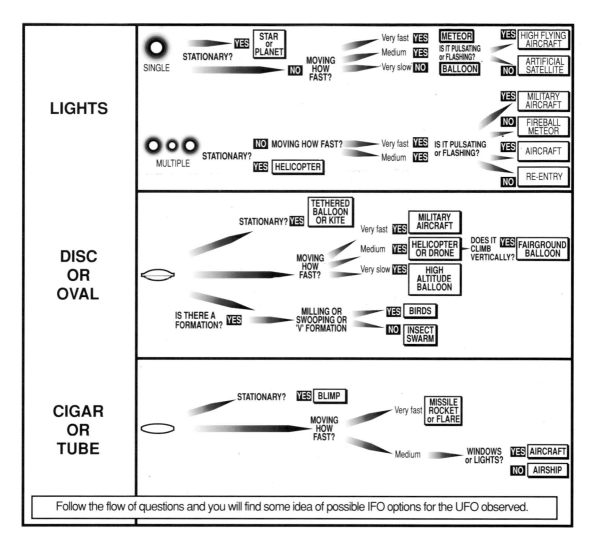

Follow the flow of questions and you will find some idea of possible IFO options for the UFO observed.

other traffic about and engines cut back the aircraft is almost gliding. If you happen to be underneath such a jet when it throttles up and switches on its full lighting once more, the transformation from ghostly glow sailing across the night to a mass of lights making a throaty roar can unnerve anybody.

⊡ Clues: *shape* (oval or cigar in daylight, ball or formation of lights at night – usually at least some are flashing); *size* (from small ball to moon); *colour* (usually white at night, but with blue, red, green all likely as well); *speed* (like speeding car, but can be slower if seen from head-on from some distance); *duration* (usually at least two or three minutes, up to about ten if seen head-on)

Airships

Although thought of as a relic from the past, airships are still around and seem to be growing in popularity. New designs take advantage of the desire for fuel economy and noise restrictions and utilize safer non-flammable gases which do not risk the disasters that ended the first reign of the airship sixty years ago.

Commercial airships do fly. In America, powered 'blimps' are often used in connection with sporting events and festivals. Some even carry electronic message boards on the side to flash out sentences. If you see these lights at night from an acute angle you cannot read what the message says, but will

An old faithful of UFOlore set to become a new demon in the sky: the airship, blimp or dirigible. They look innocent enough when floating past in clear daylight view but, at night or at odd angles, they can seem very puzzling.

see a random sequence of flashing lights that may easily create the illusion of a well-lit UFO.

Airships are simple to identify in daytime because of their unique cigar-like shape and very slow drifting motion. But new designs are bringing slightly faster speeds. At night, with unconventional lighting as well as electronic message boards, the impression is very different.

At present, there are not many airships and it should be easy to find out if one was travelling in your area (it may well have been given publicity). But the situation can change and there is a strong belief amongst UFO investigators that a secret type of advanced military airship has created some remarkable encounters with well-lit, oddly shaped and slowly drifting UFOs in the vicinity of military bases.

⊡ Clues: *shape* (oval or cigar [no wings] in daytime, multiple lights at night); *size* (at least moon-like, maybe larger); *colour* (usually white); *speed* (very slow, drifting motion); *duration* (at least several minutes)

Balloons

Hot-air balloons are easy to recognize in daytime owing to their large size, unless they are at extreme distances. Then they will behave like airships, but look smaller and like other balloon types described below. They rarely fly at night, but the most obvious clue if they do fly is the orange flame. This creates the heat needed to expand gases and lift the unseen canopy off the ground.

Hoaxers have perfected small model balloons out of simple things like plastic bags and candles. These can sail through the sky as orange glows which finally catch fire and die. As the fabric of the balloon (e.g., a bag) is lit it can melt and form a trail of burning debris that falls to earth, looking not unlike a 'stepladder' descending from the main UFO mass.

Richard Branson has cleverly developed a balloon that resembles a UFO in design and outline. This has already led to one major incident when it was tested for an abortive April Fools' stunt. A 'UFO kite' has also been built by a London inventor. While being tested, this small tethered object – made up of highly silvered parts that sparkled as it rotated in the wind well above the ground – incited numerous UFO sightings in the London area. Similar kites have provoked more sightings after wider sales.

During daylight a new type of balloon designed for fairgrounds and fêtes is matt on one side and silvered on the other. When released, these drift free and can float for hundreds of miles. Because they are relatively small they can only be seen soon after release, when near the ground, but can be easily mistaken for a large object high in the sky. On a sunny day they can seem to flash when they rotate in the wind and the silvery side catches the sunlight. When more stable they appear as metallic ovals or discs.

Weather stations and airports launch much larger balloons several times a day to test wind speeds high above the earth. These are huge silvered bags of gas which can expand as the air pressure reduces at great heights. So large are these objects that they can be seen from the ground even if they are as far away as fifty thousand feet – well above the height of most commercial aircraft. As a result, they move very slowly and take a long time to pass across the sky, looking like a tiny silver ball or daylight 'star'.

⊡ Clues: *shape* (ball or oval); *size* (from starlike point to small ball); *colour* (white, except hot-air balloons at night, which are orange); *speed* (always from almost no motion at all to very slow drifting – but a small toy balloon nearby may move faster); *duration* (from two minutes to a long time)

Searchlights

Military units often possess powerful searchlights for use during training exercises. Others can be connected with airports or police use. These project skywards and can reach the height of low cloud. The effect can be enhanced by mist or water vapour in the atmosphere. As a result an oval patch of light will form on the cloud when illuminated by the beam that is probing skyward. In the dark you may not see the source and it is easy to mistake what appears for a stationery oval craft that is projecting a beam of light down to the ground.

A more recent menace is a clever, computer-controlled series of laser-powered searchlights. These are also very powerful, shine on to cloud and are programmed to move about in a swooping, dancing motion around a fixed point. The result is a spectacular display of moving oval lights which seem to rotate around one another in the sky. They can be seen many miles from their source of projec-

tion (up to twenty-five miles in line of sight has been reliably recorded). From that distance, you are unlikely to have any idea of the source of the display (which might be a funfair, nightclub, rock concert, etc.). All you will see are a series of oddly moving white glows in the sky.

The big clue is that many people will probably report seeing them at the same time (uncommon in real UFO cases) and they will be visible for a long time (up to several hours). They may also reappear on other nights. Despite these hints, major UFO sightings provoking intense media speculation have occurred in many places during recent years. At least one town has debated banning the lights as a traffic hazard. Many people have mistaken them for UFOs and paid more attention to the skies than to the road ahead!

⊡ Clues: *shape* (oval, sometimes several ovals moving in formation); *size* (small ball or up to moon-like); *colour* (white); *speed* (mostly do not move but the new laser searchlights rotate in large arc around fixed point); *duration* (most likely to be visible for a long time – at least a few minutes)

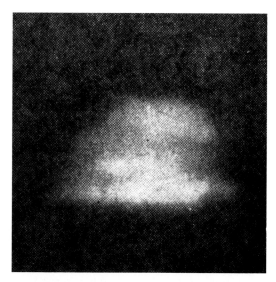

A UFO photographed over Romania which has been identified as a high-altitude weather balloon that had drifted thousands of miles. Through a telescope or binoculars, a triangular shape such as this is often in evidence as the huge airbag of silvered material expands to great size.

3 SKYWATCHING FOR UFOs

DURING THE 1960s, it was very popular to hold skywatching parties in the summer months. A group of people would visit an area where many UFOs had been seen and gaze at the skies for hours on end in the hope of seeing something fantastic.

The idea fell from favour when countless reports of UFOs, which were in reality simple lights with fairly mundane explanations, swamped investigation groups, who failed to persuade witnesses that they had not seen a UFO. But a series of co-ordinated skywatches were mounted by UFO groups during the 1970s – linking sites right across one country with walkie-talkies. The aim was to provide photographic evidence of an unexplained phenomenon. Some tantalizing results were achieved, but nothing conclusive.

However, skywatching can be a very rewarding pastime, if properly organized, and if entered into with the right expectations.

Organizing a Skywatch

Skywatching can be done on your own, but many find it more fun to organize in groups, at different sites linked by communication. Certainly there will be long periods when little is happening, so be prepared for that. Remember that if you are taking a radio or other noise-generating equipment to help pass the time you must consider the local people.

It is important to get out of a town environment. UFOs do appear over built-up locations, but evidence shows them to be far more commonplace in rural areas. This may only be because the sky is easier to see where there are few buildings blocking horizons and no artificial lighting dulling the clarity. It may also be partly due to the increased amount of time people in country areas spend looking skyward. City folk are largely unobservant. A giant UFO could drift overhead and many of them would never see it!

If you can get to one of the UFO-rich locations discussed in this book, you'll likely find it much more rewarding. Of course, some are very remote and others only produce UFO sightings at certain times of the year. The Hessdalen lights are seen

Some of the best skywatches ever mounted were staged in terrible weather by UFO groups in Scandinavia under the Project Hessdalen banner. Their patience in stalking out a UFO-haunted site was often rewarded. Many strange light phenomena have appeared in the Norwegian valley.

in a valley near the Arctic Circle during the winter when the local temperature rarely even rises up to freezing. Yet dedicated skywatching teams have monitored the area with amazing equipment and obtained some of the best UFO evidence ever gathered. In Britain, one skywatch was co-ordinated with the local-airport radar operators to track down an IFO.

However, you do not need such determination. If there is no site near you, then select one by studying maps. A good place to go – especially for your first watch, when you will want to see things – is on a hill overlooking an airport or military base. Other things that might produce IFOs and keep you awake are chemical factories, electricity-generating

stations (where odd electrical effects might appear) and unlit roads crossing hills (car headlights on these can look like UFOs up in the sky).

A hilly area is always the best vantage point for a skywatch. Later on you might want to increase your expectations by moving away from positions with countless IFO possibilities to areas which our UFO knowledge suggest might trigger real sightings. If you can read a geological map or consult a friendly geologist, find a hill slope overlooking a valley or plain through which a fault-line runs.

These fractures below the earth's surface are what sometimes cause earthquakes – but far more often seem to be tied in with less destructive UFO sightings. Locations near quarries, dams and new

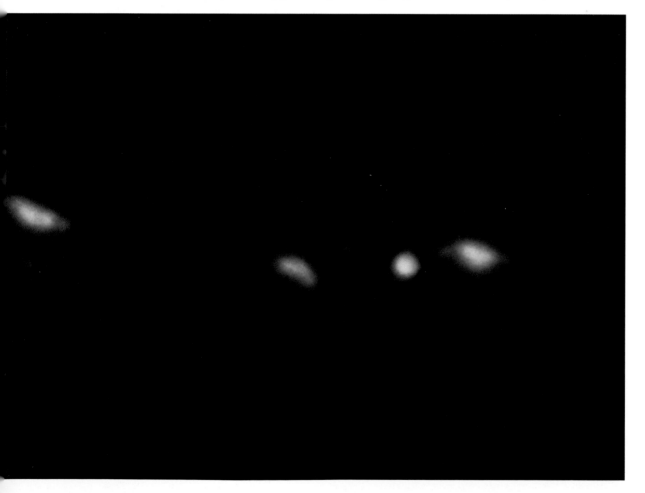

road excavations are excellent places to look.

Also, while you do not want to choose a night with bad weather, if you can organize a watch at short notice, another good time to plan one is straight after a spell of bad weather, when the skies are clearing and fresh, bright conditions are arriving. The frontal pressure systems responsible for this change can spring UFO-active areas into life.

If all else fails then pick a night near the full moon, as this is also thought by some to help increase UFO activity. You will at least be able to watch the moon rise and set, and see how passing clouds can alter its appearance.

Of course, you must always remember to check you are not on private land, and seek permission if you are – especially if camping or lighting a fire. Never leave litter or disturb the surroundings for future visitors.

Recording Results

Night watches are by far the most productive. Over three-quarters of all sightings occur between ten p.m. and seven a.m. In fact, there is a little known peak of UFO activity at around three a.m., which no researcher has yet been able to explain. This was discovered in many statistical studies of sighting totals.

Wrap up warmly and take some food and hot drinks; more specifically you need as many of the following as possible:

☐ A *flashlight* to illuminate what will be very dark surroundings;
☐ A *watch* or clock to record the accurate times of all activity;
☐ *Binoculars* equipped for night viewing (but remember they can distort images);
☐ At least one *camera* (see below for more details of photography);
☐ A selection of *small coins* and other common objects (a dried pea is a handy size) to hold at arms' length and gauge sizes of objects seen against them;

☐ A *thermometer* to record air temperature at half-hourly intervals.

In order to log your observations, you will also need a small ruled notebook – pocket-size – and a couple of pens, of course, in case one runs out! In the left margin write the time you start the watch, the time of all temperature readings (and it is a good idea to note all significant changes in the weather – e.g., the amount of cloud cover, changes in wind speed or direction, etc.), plus the time when you make any entry into the book.

You should record everything that looks noteworthy, describing what you saw in as much detail as it takes. You may well see aircraft, meteors, odd clouds, animals; in fact, many things. Even if you recognize them for what they are put them down. One of the best outcomes of a skywatch is to increase your ability to recognize IFOs. Even if you never see a UFO (but there is every chance you will) the skywatch is an excellent training ground for your powers of discrimination. Never forget that about ninety-five per cent of all UFO sightings are really IFOs – so the next time someone tells you they saw a UFO, chances are that it was something identifiable and, based on skywatching experience, you might be able to solve their particular riddle.

If you can take a small battery-operated tape recorder with you, do so. Describing what you see, at what time, on to this is much easier than writing long notes in the dark. And if you see a UFO, your recording is great evidence!

Checking Your Results

You should carry this book with you on skywatches, so that anything puzzling can be compared with the IFO descriptions on pages 36–49.

You may later want to call local airports or air bases for help – to see if they have recorded anything that night for themselves. Remember they are busy and rarely have the time to assist callers. It may be better, if you are really baffled, to send a copy of what you have recorded to one of the responsible UFO groups you will find listed at the end of this book. They may well be able to make such checks for you.

Details of weather records and balloon releases are harder to come by, but a bona-fide UFO group may have established connections that make it easier for them to obtain such material.

If you have a local astronomical association (the Yellow Pages or telephone directory should help in such quests), then they will assist any responsible plea for help to find a possible astronomical solution to your sighting. Again, most major UFO groups have astronomical consultants for just this purpose. It is even possible to buy inexpensive software for most types of home computers that allow you to enter the exact date, time and location of your sighting and so generate a map of the sky. This will tell you if there were any bright stars or planets where your 'UFO' appeared.

Of course, such programmes cannot include meteors, fireballs or space junk re-entries – as these are less predictable.

Photographing Skywatches

Take two cameras, if at all possible. One should have a standard lens, and the other a telephoto for close-ups. Do not use a flash, as this will only spoil the picture and cannot illuminate an object in the sky. You can purchase special films for use in low light that will help compensate for the dark conditions, but if you use such film it will be very grainy so try to compromise somewhere in between low- and normal-light film.

A tripod to steady your shot will overcome one of the most common problems of skywatch photographs. As light is so dim, the shutter must stay open for a relatively long time. It is impossible not to jerk the camera during this time, if you hold it by hand, and that will spoil the results.

Although it is very difficult in darkened skies and rural surroundings, if at all possible try to get something other than the UFO in shot – even clouds may help. Otherwise, it is very difficult to conduct

Being airborne is a good way to investigate phenomena, notably crop circles. But it can be productive for UFO sightings, too. This object was photographed from an aircraft flying over Japan.

photographic analysis – especially if no scale can be determined.

Another very useful thing to do is to take comparison shots of the sky without the UFO present – but immediately after it has left. Use the same camera on the same settings. Also photograph the same scene as soon as it is light, without switching the camera position or the setting of the lens. In this way the UFO can be exactly located on the background scenery.

Make a careful note of when each photograph is taken and full details of all the settings of the camera; these are very important.

If you think that you may have photographed a UFO, resist the temptation to have the film processed at the local store. If you have your own processing facilities, use them. Poor developing can ruin a UFO film. For best results, contact a UFO group immediately, but do not send the original negatives through the post. They will arrange to collect these and give you a full receipt.

Many witnesses lose the negatives, thinking they are of limited value. But for the purpose of scientific study of UFO photographs the negatives are far more important than a print of the image. So do look after them.

4 THE MOST UFO-HAUNTED PLACES IN THE WORLD

Africa

The Canary Islands

THE CANARY ISLANDS off the north-west coast of the African continent, are of Spanish dependency and have a warm, little-changing climate all year round which attracts tourists. They are formed from volcanic rock and on Lanzarote, recently active volcanoes are still found – evidenced by rich black soil.

Local legend has it that this group of seven main islands are the original source of the Atlantis myth – a civilization in the Atlantic which reputedly had incredibly advanced knowledge. Ancient writings say it vanished beneath the waves several million years ago, when a huge volcanic eruption took place. Indeed, so desolate are some of the landscapes on the islands that science-fiction films have used them to portray other worlds.

Ironically, other worlds may have more than a passing interest in the Canaries, as many extraordinary UFO sightings have been recorded from here.

On the evening of 22 June 1976, a Spanish naval corvette – the *Atrevida*, just east of the southern coast of Fuerteventura – spotted a vivid yellow light

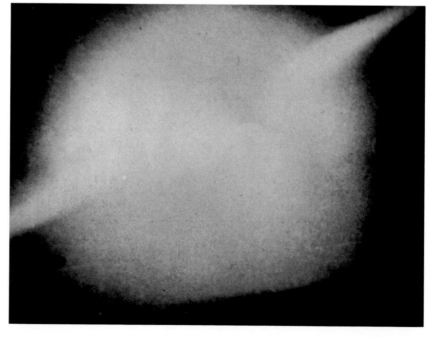

One of the photographs obtained during the major Canary Islands UFO encounter in 1976. The huge orb of light was seen by thousands of people and was photographed at Maspalomas on Gran Canaria. The pictures were released by the Spanish Air Force, who could not explain the event.

with a blue tinge. It was seen to rise from the vicinity of Punta Lantailla and then drop a curtain of light towards the ground, which illuminated both sea and shore. The light appeared to corkscrew upwards from this halo and move away across the island towards Gran Canaria. The mass of light left by the object remained in the sky for almost forty minutes.

Three minutes after first sighting it was above Gran Canaria where residents saw it pass. A doctor travelling to see a patient near Galdar and Agaete in the north reported a huge soap bubble, containing tall figures in one-piece suits. A bluish gas filled the object inside, it developed a yellow/white spindle-like halo, whistled and headed west towards Tenerife.

At Maspalomas on Gran Canaria a witness obtained a photograph of the object. Scientists at the Monte Izane Astrophysics Observatory saw it as well and were unable to identify the phenomenon. The Air Ministry subsequently issued a report on all of this evidence and confirmed they had themselves tracked the object on radar. Five

The imposing spectacle of Mount Teide on Tenerife. UFO sightings have been made from the summit, which can be reached for a skywatch. An excellent view over the UFO-rich Canary Islands is afforded.

days later the commander of the Canary Islands Air Force, General Carlos Cavero, said publicly, 'I have for some time held the view that the UFOs are extraterrestrial craft [but] it is as difficult for official quarters to admit that something exists as it is for the church to affirm that this or that is a miracle'.

Some sceptics have suggested that this sighting involved a submarine rocket launch. Exhaust gases could create a cloud as reported. However, presumably the Spanish Air Force would know about such a launch. Spanish researcher Javier Sierra points out that this was a busy shipping zone and a submarine rocket test would be unthinkable in those circumstances.

Something remarkably similar happened again on 5 March 1979. This was also photographed – from Gran Canaria and Tenerife. An object spiralled up into the air from beneath the sea and for thirty minutes a glowing cloud of light was left in its wake. At least three sets of photographs exist for this event – including one taken by a radio engineer on the top of the tall and imposing peak of Mount Teide.

These are only some of the sightings that have made these islands an exciting place for would-be UFO witnesses to visit. Indeed, by some there is speculation about the existence of an underwater UFO base in the surrounding ocean.

Mount Teide on Tenerife can be reached by visitors and you can also get to the summit by cable car or a long, very steep walk. Arranging a sky-watch here at night would not be advisable without special permission, and many of the coastal areas are now developed for tourism. Better to choose a more remote coastal inlet or one of the many smaller peaks.

Lanzarote may be a better choice. It is the most northerly of the islands, less well developed and with plenty of open, fresh air. Yet it is readily accessible through short inter-island air and sea routes, and can now be reached directly by air from some European cities.

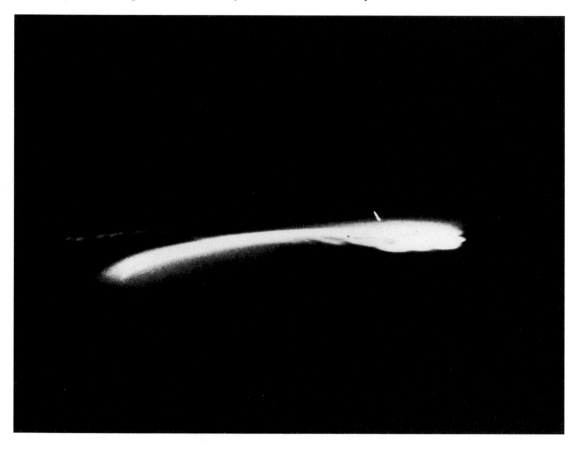

In 1979 there was an even more incredible repeat performance over the islands. Several independent sets of photographs were taken of a yellow-orange cloud that illuminated the sky after a rocketlike projectile shot into the air. Was this a secret missile test? This is one photograph taken by a British tourist at Los Gigantos, Tenerife.

North America

The Niagara Region

This area covers south-eastern Ontario in Canada, and north-western New York in America. It encircles Lake Ontario and in its hub sits the huge natural spectacle of Niagara Falls. Vast amounts of electricity and hydro-electric power are generated by the cataracts, perhaps significantly.

UFOs are known to appear in the vicinity of power stations and electricity pylons. Some argue that this is because they are natural electrical phenomena and others feel that they draw motive power from our circuits. Either way, this region has had more than its share of encounters.

At Cherry Creek, New York, just south of Buffalo, the major American city in the area, a dairy farm suffered real problems on 19 August 1956. A tractor powering milking machines stopped working. The radio began to crackle with static and a red oval shape landed nearby. A bull tethered to a metal pole became so agitated that it bent the pole through forty-five degrees in its attempt to flee. The UFO took off skyward and left the clouds with a strange green hue. A peculiar odour also filled the air. Both the state police and eventually the US Air Force visited the site, but could not explain what had happened. But they did find some unusual viscous liquid on the ground. This was purple in colour and could not be identified.

In January 1958, close to Niagara Falls, on the American side of the border, a woman driving in a snowstorm found her car engine and lights fading, then failing altogether. A large object appeared ahead with two shadowy beings beside it. The object began to rotate and then flew into the air. The car now worked normally, but the witness found a hole melted in the snow at the landing spot

The raw electricity-generating power of Niagara Falls on the US/Canada border seems to act like a magnet for UFO sightings.

and the grass underneath was warm to the touch.

Things have also happened across the Canadian border. On 2 August 1979, a group of witnesses followed some arrowhead shapes on to land owned by Ontario Hydro, east of Toronto. They were actually hovering low down above the electricity powerlines. Various other objects seen in the same area include a cigar covered by a green haze and humming like a generator.

A few days later, again on Ontario Hydro's land, a teenaged girl felt a hypnotic compulsion to walk into a field after a UFO sighting. All sounds of the environment faded away – a symptom commonly reported by witnesses to close encounters and called the 'Oz Factor'. It seems to signify that an altered state of consciousness has been entered. The girl recovered her senses on the grass after a few minutes of missing time. The UFO was gone.

Subsequent investigation by the Canadian UFO Research Network found an area of depressed grass at the site, as if something had landed. Even after a heavy rain storm, radiation levels higher than the normal background count were taken beside this flattened area.

The teenager was put under regression hypnosis and relived an apparent abduction experience in which she was taken into the landed object and medically examined. Blood was reputedly extracted without pain from her finger, which had an unexplained pinprick hole.

Another abduction occurred in October 1971, when a rock group were kidnapped from their van near St Catherine's, a city by the Falls. A decade later, hypnotic research was carried out by a New York psychiatrist which revealed an astonishing tale of life-long contact. It began in 1957 when the band leader was abducted from his pushchair at the age of two. The entities were small, with large, slanting eyes, and they conducted genetic experiments.

This sequence of close encounters and their links with the Falls and electricity has led some to believe that UFOs might have triggered the amazing power-blackout of 9 November 1965. Much of New York State and part of Ontario suffered an extensive loss of power. It was the greatest electric power failure in history. Twenty-six million people were stranded as a result.

Initially, it was thought that a relay at Clay, near Syracuse, New York, was to blame. Interestingly at the exact time of power loss the pilot and passenger in a small aircraft nearby saw a red oval object above the powerlines. The chairman of the local power company stated after the catastrophic failure that 200,000 kilowatts were routinely downloaded from Niagara: but, 'Suddenly we didn't have it . . . it just wasn't there.'

The infamous 'Condon' study tried to scotch claims that a UFO had caused this event; quoting from the final report by the American power commission. This went to great lengths tracing the origin of the problem to a sudden overload in a back-up relay at a power station on the Niagara river, which runs into the Falls. But its key words are really: 'The precise cause of the back-up relay energization is not known.'

In other words, a UFO might still have been the source of what became an incredible series of tripping relays, which toppled like dominoes in a very long line, one after the other.

Obviously, the Niagara area promises to be a good spot for UFO watching. The immediate region around the Falls is now very commercialized, with many helicopter pleasure flights. There are several very high vantage points here, nonetheless. Prospects are better from one of the more rural areas on the southern shore of Lake Ontario, but the land lies lower.

The North-West Frontier

The modern UFO mystery began in the summer of 1947, not just with Kenneth Arnold's sighting near Mount Rainier, but a series of encounters from the Cascade range. The deeply symbolic UFO elements in the surreal American television series 'Twin Peaks' – set and filmed in this region – are no coincidence.

This chain of still volcanic mountains lies on the active fault zone between two continental plates. These are like massive reed mats of crust floating on the molten earth and as they rub against one

One of the two famous photographs taken in May 1950 at McMinnville, Oregon, and still widely considered amongst the most important in the world. They were taken by a farming couple and show a large, distant object of unexplained origin that displays the effect of dust in the intervening air.

another they generate friction, heat and, therefore, earthquakes and eruptions.

To the south, in California, the San Andreas Fault is responsible for the destructive tremors that strike. UFO researchers recognize a connection between seismic activity and sightings, so it is not surprising that the state has created numerous encounters – for example, in the Tujunga Canyon area of the San Gabriel mountains to the east of Pasedena.

However, in the extreme western states of Oregon and Washington volcanoes are the real problem. The awesome detonation of Mount St Helen's in 1980 is a ready reminder of the raw

power trapped beneath the rocks and may well help to explain why this is such a UFO-active location.

Undoubtedly, this is also one of the best places in the world for photographing UFOs. Two of the most evidential cases on record come from the mountainous region south of Portland.

Possibly the most important is that taken by farming couple Paul Trent and his wife, in McMinnville to the west of the Williamette River.

It was 11 May 1950 when Mrs Trent pointed out to her husband a disclike craft with a flat base. He took two photographs before it disappeared. The images were clear and sharp, with plenty of foreground detail and obvious effects of mist demon-

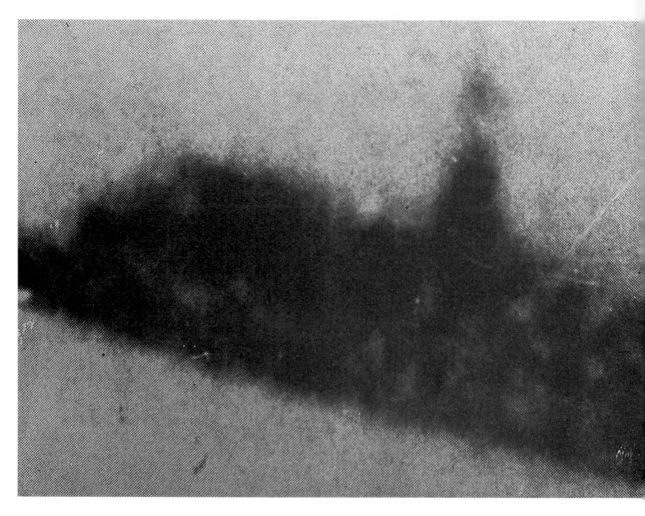

strating the distance of the object from the camera.

Yet the Trents did not seek to use them to make money. They sat in the camera until the film was used up and later became public knowledge only by accident. The Trents thought they had seen an unusual new aircraft, although no known craft then (or now) looked or behaved as this object did.

Through the years, extensive investigation has been conducted and nobody has satisfactorily dented the evidence. It was the one photographic case that did not show cracks after months of intensive study by scientists from the Colorado University project. Dr William Hartmann's analysis offers little doubt that the most realistic option was what he called an 'extraordinary flying object, silvery, metallic, disc-shaped, tens of metres in diameter and evidently artificial'.

This case alone may vindicate the reality of UFOs, which is why every effort has been made to explain it in some other way. It is one of the few to have been tested exhaustively by computer enhancement methods developed out of the NASA space programme. It passed without reservation.

Another classic case comes from a witness with quite the opposite background to the Trents – he was a college professor with a PhD in biochemistry who was certainly not after notoriety. He had driven along the Williamette Pass south-east of McMinnville and up into the mountains. From five thousand feet at the Diamond Peak viewing area he took a series of pictures of the rugged scenery, with snow coating the fir trees spread out down below.

60

It was 22 November 1966 and after taking his photographs he caught sight of something fuzzy out of the corner of his eye. He took one more quick photograph before it vanished skyward. Uncertain if he had really seen anything, the doctor left the film in the camera until the roll was developed. When it was processed something very unexpected had appeared.

There was a disc-shaped object with a flat base – but in three different places at once! Some were suspicious that he did not 'see' this at the time. UFO expert Adrian Vance argued otherwise. His complex study noted that the shutter of the camera was open for a fraction of a second. If the UFO were 'phasing' in and out of reality this would be captured. Our eyes cannot react to rapid changes.

◄ An enlargement of the McMinnville image showing its unusual design. Many attempts have been made to analyse the photograph and prove it wanting. But it has come through all tests set before it and is regarded by virtually all informed commentators as a real UFO.

▲ Taken in the same UFO-haunted region of the North-West Frontier this startling shot was captured at Williamette Pass, Oregon in 1966. Three images appear in a single frame as the UFO rises from the snow-clad trees, sucking a plume beneath it. Evidence suggests the object may have faded in and out of reality whilst the shutter was open.

The awesome natural spectacle of the canyonlands in Arizona and New Mexico. Is the geological power inherent within such areas a clue to the number of UFOs that appear? Some researchers feel that it is.

They 'see' a continuous moving image.

Vance's calculations indicate that the object was some twenty-two feet in diameter and rising from a clearing. It seemed to suck a plume of snow from the tree tops beneath. It displayed what UFO researchers call a 'falling leaf' motion, but in reverse. If you drop a saucer into a bowl of water you will see the same effect. It moves in smooth zig-zags, due to its shape and the flow of water. Witnesses have often reported UFOs exhibiting this effect but the Williamette Pass photograph is the first that displays it.

Because there are three separate images rather than a blur of motion, Vance says that the UFO must have also faded in and out of our time space and disappeared – then reappeared twice while the camera shutter was open.

If this is a correct assessment and the photograph is genuine, then it may be even more important than the one at McMinnville, for it proves that UFOs behave in a manner completely outside that of normal physical craft; although, interestingly, its motion is not unlike what we have recently learnt to be occurring at the quantum level of sub-atomic physics. Here ghost particles *do* fade in and out of reality in rapid succession.

UFO-watching from this area is a delight, with many beautiful mountain locations and excellent long-range views. Even from one of the main roads through the mountains, traffic is almost non-existent at night and won't interfere with your plans.

Another good location is south-west of the town of Yakima, which is just north of Portland and into Washington State. Yakima was the airstrip where Kenneth Arnold first landed in June 1947 to set off the UFO mystery, but the area has known many UFOs. Researcher Greg Long has studied the events on the Indian reservation in the vicinity of White Swan and Toppenish. During the period from 1972 to 1974 there was intensive activity, often witnessed by well-trained fire wardens from tall observation towers.

Most of the phenomena witnessed south of Yakima comprises balls of light – often orange or yellow, which can split apart, bounce along the ground or turn into peculiar misty clouds. There are reports of lights following cars on the quiet roads and in some cases of both engine and lights cutting out at closest proximity, as in similar encounters all over the world.

Given that this is an Indian reservation, special permission should be sought to skywatch here and the weather can be harsh in the autumn and winter when the lights are most common. If you can get the help of the wardens in the various high towers during a properly organized skywatch you may increase your chances of success.

The Texas Triangle

If you take a triangle of land with sides approximately 180 miles long between Lubbock and Alpine in western Texas and Albuquerque in New Mexico you will find a lot of desert and canyon land, but very little else and certainly not many people. However, you will also have demarked an area which contains half a dozen of the most significant UFO events in the history of the subject.

A UFO over the Texas Triangle? Typical border country with a strange object hovering above the hill. But, in fact, this is just a processing mark on the negative!

Already described in the first part of this book is the alleged 1947 crash outside of Roswell (some say closer to Corona, New Mexico), the amazing series of car stoppages around Levelland, Texas in 1957, and the landing of an object with entities witnessed in 1964 by a police officer at Socorro, New Mexico.

There are plenty of other incidents. Indeed, between 1947 and 1952 so much went on in the area that grave concern was expressed by the American government. Much secret research takes place here; e.g., at the missile sites and early atomic bomb-test locations of White Sands near Alomogordo. Holloman Air Force base, where aliens are alleged to have landed in 1971, is also here. Mysterious green fireballs that behave completely unlike meteors led the famous meteor expert, Dr Lincoln La Paz, to expend much time on them. They

appeared during those early years in various places – such as near Vaughn, New Mexico. A number of recently released documents show the seriousness with which the security agencies took them.

The photograph on the cover of this book was taken in the area on 16 October 1957 by a nurse on the Indian reservation at Three Rivers, southwest of Roswell. The glowing white oval seen in daylight was hovering above a restricted area. There has been much speculation about this being a lenticular cloud formed above the Sacramento Mountains. However, some experts insist that it reflects too much light to be a cloud, even though its stationary appearance supports that contention.

This was just a few days before the wave of sightings that occurred to the east, around Levelland. Apart from the sequence of car stoppages during the night of 2 and 3 November, there were

other similar cases, including several in the vicinity of the Sacramento Mountains themselves.

At Orogrande, on the same road and about thirty miles south of where the 'cloud' photograph was taken less than three weeks earlier, an electronics engineer lost radio, lights and then engine on his car at 1 p.m. on 4 November. Several other cars on the road also stopped as an oval object approached from the vicinity of the mountains to the north and flew over the road. As it did so, the engineer felt waves of heat. Later his skin became red and itchy on all the exposed parts of his body.

Just a few miles away, again on the same road, a couple driving at 9.20 a.m. on 7 November saw another strange object which appeared to affect the speedometer readings on their instrument panel.

Both of these events are very near Las Cruces where, in 1948, famed astronomer, Dr Clyde Tom-baugh, observed an oval-shaped object with windows, and a blue-green glow, as did his wife and mother-in-law.

It is often said by sceptics that UFOs cannot be real, as astronomers never report them. This is, of course, nonsense. Recall that the first photograph of a UFO in Mexico came from an astronomer – and Tombaugh was reportedly baffled by what he saw. As the man who discovered the planet Pluto he is one of the most celebrated in his field.

More classic photographs (a series of five) were taken at Lubbock, Texas, on 31 August 1951, featuring a V-shaped formation of lights that passed over the area. In fact, the 'lights' had first been seen several days before by a remarkable group of college professors who were sat talking in their garden. They included an engineer, geologist and physicist – all of whom could not explain the lights which silently swept over with an eerie blue-green glow and then returned later.

As explained in the IFO section of this book, formations of UFOs are now immediately considered suspect by investigators. Indeed, there was a good deal of talk that the Lubbock lights were birds (possibly plover) reflecting the mercury streetlighting from their underbellies. The explanation has been widely dismissed and was confused by the official US Air Force investigator, Captain Edward Ruppelt. Normally a perceptive UFOlogist shackled by military protocol, after leaving the air force he wrote in his 1956 book that he had thought the Lubbock lights were birds, but was wrong. He now knew the answer was a mundane one but could not reveal it.

Yet, we now know these lights without any doubt *were* birds. In fact, despite the claims to the contrary, still in many UFO books, one of the professors (aptly named Dr Ducker) proved this as long ago as 1952.

When the lights returned in the late summer of 1952 Ducker carried out a remarkable series of complex experiments, described to local journalist David Wheeler in 1977. These eventually established that the lights were unquestionably flocks of birds reflecting streetlights. Even so, he still believed that there were other, still unresolved, happenings in the Texas Triangle area.

A black-and-white print of the Ella Fortune photograph taken in the Texas Triangle (for a colour version see the cover of this book). The picture was obtained on October 1957, south of Alamogordo, New Mexico, near the Holloman Air Force base and close by the site of the first atomic explosion in history in 1945. Some say it is a lenticular cloud, others a balloon. But its origin has never been established.

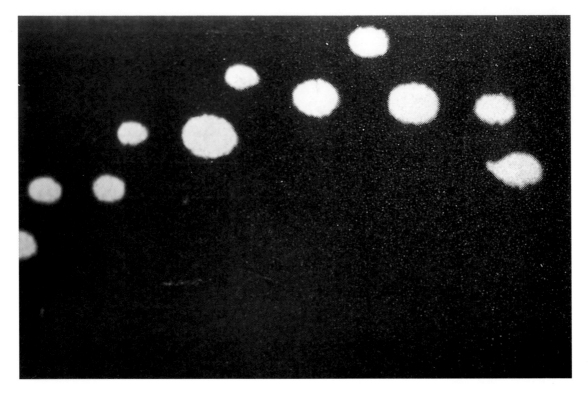

The famous Lubbock lights, as photographed over the Texas town by Carl Hart Junior in August 1951. They have been the subject of controversy ever since, but their origin as a natural phenomenon is now assured.

This area is not an easy one to visit for a skywatch. The desert can be very inhospitable with its wide temperature swings. But if you can base yourself in Albuquerque (a modern city rising like an oasis) then you are amid one of the most dramatic areas on earth for UFO activity.

To the south, around Marfa, west of Alpine, in Texas, is one of the most famous areas in the world for lights in the sky. The Marfa lights have danced above the Chinati Mountains for centuries and their presence is even marked by a roadside plaque on US Highway 90 between the two towns, some seven miles east of Marfa near an abandoned air base.

The lights are yellowish in colour and theories have suggested that they may be optical refractions of car lights on distant mountain roads. But several experiments have seemingly ruled this out and the lights are a popular tourist attraction, given their very regular appearance at night.

Journalist and researcher with the group MUFON (Mutual UFO Network), Dennis Stacy has traced several reports where the lights appeared to display 'intelligence', as if following cars and people, but are rarely anything more substantial than glowing blobs. Even so this very flat location east of Marfa with clean air and high expectations offer a good point for a skywatch if time is limited.

The Gulf Strip

In the late 1980s, one town in America became synonymous with UFOs. That was the otherwise obscure but pleasantly named Gulf Breeze. Deriving this name from the Gulf of Mexico it sits on an off-shore sand strip across the estuary from Pensacola, Florida, a port at the far western edge of the state. This is part of a hundred-mile stretch full of UFO tales, which ranges east from Biloxi in Mississippi, through the entire coast of Alabama and on toward the Gulf seaside region with its famed naval base.

During a major wave of UFO sightings in October 1973, the Mississippi town of Pascagoula (twenty-five miles east of Biloxi) experienced one of the most frightening close encounters then known. Two men fishing off the pier heard a buzzing sound and saw a blue glowing object descend behind them. Strange creatures with wrinkled skins and pincer-like hands emerged and an abduction followed. The men were dumped back outside the object with only hazy memories of what occurred.

A major police investigation failed to crack their story. They were even left alone with a tape recorder, unbeknown to them, in the hope that they would incriminate themselves. They did not. In a public appearance fourteen years later one of the men revealed how he had turned down huge sums of money to make a movie of his story, because money was not what the experience was about. It was something much deeper than that.

After this encounter, the Mississippi and Alabama area was swamped with close encounters. A police officer at Falkville actually photographed a strange figure in a silver suit that he chased (and lost) in his patrol car, when responding to a UFO sighting. On the very same night (17 October 1973) police were busy investigating the tale of a man driving on the coastal Interstate Highway 10 between Mobile, Alabama and Pensacola. He claimed that his pick-up truck was attacked by an object from the sky and sucked inside a UFO where he was examined by six small entities. Police appeared satisfied that he was telling the truth.

Such precedents led the way for the amazing happenings in Gulf Breeze, which began on 11 November 1987 when local businessman 'Ed' Walters took the first in a series of photographs of a structured object with windows or portholes. It was more graphic in design than anything seen since Adamski's contentious pictures over thirty years earlier.

As Walters took more and more photographs, each showing near identical craft, he also alleged closer encounters. These ranged from being fired upon by a beam of light, hiding under his truck as a UFO landed on the road (which he photographed) and an entity that he chased away from his house

(but did not photograph). He also appeared to undergo an abduction where some investigators claimed an 'implant' was placed into his head. But before this could be searched for with a hospital CAT scan device, he underwent another experience which some argue was a second abduction made to remove the implant and stop its discovery by UFOlogists.

UFO investigators flocked to the area and in summer 1990 even held a major conference there with full media fanfare. 'Ed' had meanwhile written a best-selling book about his experiences and a TV movie was being made to depict the story. Leading UFOlogists stood by him, pointing out that his photographs passed analytical tests and that when given special cameras to use he still produced photographs. Others hotly disputed this, some uncovering what they claimed was evidence of trickery. A war of bitter words was unleashed within UFOlogy which still rumbles on; at one stage there was even the discovery of designs for model UFOs in Ed's old home and a confession to police by a man who said he helped set up the hoax. Both stories were flatly denounced by Walters and by some of the UFOlogists involved.

Those who backed the case cited as prime evidence the fact that other photographs of Ed-like UFOs were taken in the area by other (anonymous) people and that many other witnesses had publicly come forward to say they had seen odd lights in the sky.

Gulf Breeze soon became a real tourist centre for UFO spotters. Dozens were skywatching on most nights. On 20 June 1991 a group of fourteen watchers observed and photographed two bright lights that appeared in the sky for a few seconds, turned red and then vanished. Some investigators speculated that these could be naval flares, but the controversy continues unabated.

These pictures were taken from the southern end of the Pensacola Bay Bridge, which links the town with the Gulf Breeze area. It offers a fine view of open sky and is considered the best place in the area to look for UFOs. For the time being, at least, on most nights you are assured of human company. As for there being non-human company as well . . . who knows?

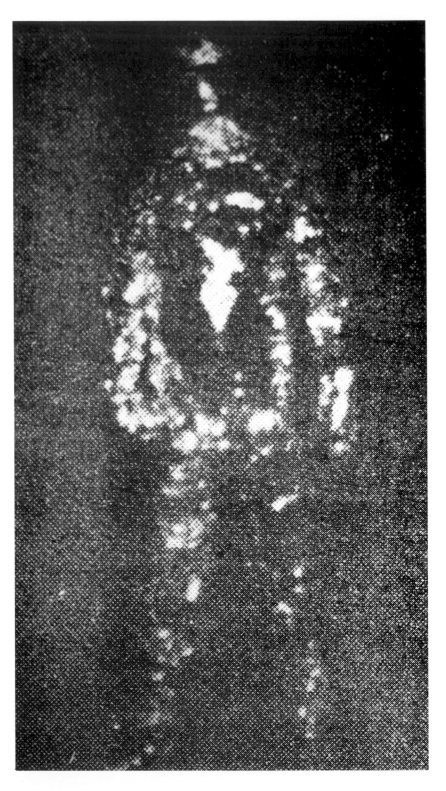

During a major wave in the Gulf Strip in October 1973 police officer Jeff Greenhaw got a call late one night at Falkville, Alabama to investigate a UFO sighting. He saw no UFO, but instead confronted this tall figure in a silver suit which he was able to photograph. It ran into the dark and he gave chase in his squad car but lost it.

South America

The Sao José, Brazil Mountains

When looking for UFOs in South America it may be worthwhile asking a local, 'Do you know the way to Sao José?' This region in the mountains three hundred miles north-west of the Brazilian city of Sao Paulo is a haven for UFO watchers.

Legends go back hundreds of years throughout this immense country. Cynthia Luce has reported what happened when she bought a remote house in Sao José do Rio Preto. She was told it was 'haunted' by lights known locally as the 'mother of gold'. The legend was that these yellow-orange globes would lead you to the best place to dig for treasure.

Possibly this story has a basis in fact. The hills are heavily faulted and contain mineral ores. If these UFOs are geophysical phenomena (earthlights, as researcher Paul Devereux calls them), then they may well be more common over geological regions with precious metal deposits.

Cynthia Luce first saw the lights in June 1980, but they have drifted around the village many times since. They often appear to respond to human presence, as if displaying intelligence, and have been noted in waves. However, rather more than lights have been seen in this region over the years. It has one of the highest concentrations of claimed abduction (or attempted alien kidnappings) anywhere in the world.

Indeed, what is widely regarded as the first modern abduction – the extraordinary story of Antonio Villas Boas – took place at Sao Francisco de Sales, only about sixty miles north-west on 15 October 1957. Villas Boas reported being abducted from his fields by a beautiful but strange-looking woman who yelped like a dog. She forced him to have intercourse after which she signalled in a ges-

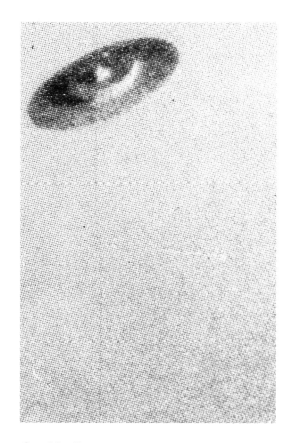

One of Brazil's most contentious UFO photographs, part of a series of five taken in May 1952 at Barra da Tijuca. The platelike object flew over the rocky hillside on a sunny day, but sceptics have claimed that the shadows shown on trees indicate that the sunlight was illuminating them from the opposite direction to the light on the UFO. This suggested to scientific analysts, eg, in the Condon Report, that the photographs were faked by superimposing two negatives. However, some UFOlogists point out that for this the sun would have to shine from an impossible angle. The witness hâs merely suggested that the sceptics go to the area and see for themselves how the shadows on the pictures are appropriate.

69

A celebrated colour image taken in the Andes mountains of South America, near Yungay in Peru in March 1967. Unfortunately the area was wiped out soon after by a major geological catastrophe and all traces, and the photographer, were lost.

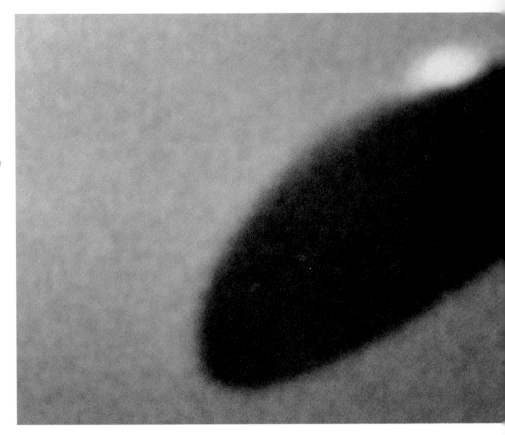

ture seeming to indicate that she would have his baby in outer space! This deeply investigated case was the first known appearance of the now common trend in abduction stories that the aliens are performing genetic or hybrid experimentation with humans.

At Catanduva, thirty miles south of Cynthia Luce's home, a case occurred on 22 May 1973, which is very typical of the dramatic local sightings. At three a.m. a travelling salesman was on his way home from Itajobi in a heavy rainstorm when his radio, then his engine began to fail. A blue beam from the sky penetrated the car. Assuming a truck was coming, he managed to steer the car off the road but no other vehicle appeared.

Jumping out in panic the man was smothered by an overpowering heat as the blue beam shone on to him. It was emerging from an opaque oval shape in the sky, out of which a tube or funnel was appearing.

Beginning to lose consciousness the witness noted, quite remarkably, that the beam had made his car look transparent. His skin was also burning. He stumbled away but collapsed on to the ground, only to be discovered some hours later by two people in a passing car. They quickly drove into town and brought the police, fearing the man must have been in an accident and was dead. But the three were able to awaken the stricken witness, who responded in terror, screaming that they were aliens!

In his semi-conscious state the man was convinced that the dark shapes he saw around him came from the UFO. He was taken to hospital and kept in for observation, after which he was eventually released with no ill-effects. But several days later, strange blotches appeared on his skin around his abdomen. Back in hospital the investigating doctor admitted he could not explain what had happened but said the man was in no way deranged.

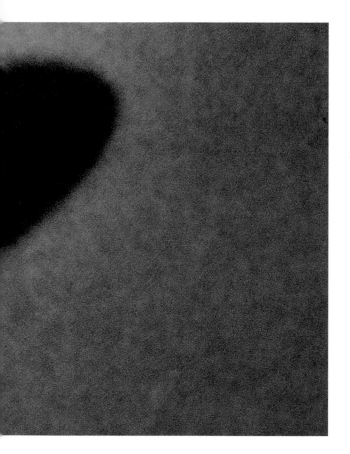

when he resisted. He began to float but recovered awareness inside a strange craft. Later investigation found his footprints leading out of the showerroom and stopping suddenly.

Under hypnotic regression it was revealed that the witness claimed to have had forced intercourse with a red-haired, naked female in a very similar manner to the Villas Boas case twenty years earlier. He was told that a male child would be born and used for experiments. The same witness claimed several later abductions which continued into the middle of the 1980s, and he had burn marks and strange cuts on his skin as apparent evidence of this.

Whether you believe abductions are real, physical events, bizarre psychological states or hallucinations triggered by unexplained natural energy emissions (the three main rival theories), they are obviously not an enviable plight. Therefore this is not the ideal area to contemplate skywatching, and in addition, its remoteness will make that difficult. However, if you feel tempted, Cynthia Luce notes that the 'mother of gold' lights are most common in the evening during the dry winter months of April to October. But it is best not to venture into here alone . . .

Bahia Blanca, Argentina

Argentina is the second most active part of the South American continent when it comes to UFOs. One of the best places to look for them is in the surroundings of the industrial city of Bahia Blanca on the northern coast. Although sightings have occurred more recently, their hey-day was in the mid seventies when strange things were constantly being reported.

One of the oddest tales came from a mechanic driving on the road east from Medanos into Bahia Blanca during the early hours of 27 August 1972. He picked up a strange hitchhiker, who gave unintelligible replies to any questions posed, until suddenly the car headlights failed and the vehicle pulled to a halt in front of a craft just sitting on the roadway

Dr Chediak reported, 'I am absolutely sure that the man is telling the truth. . . . He was burnt, and they are no ordinary burns. They look as if caused by strange rays.'

A year later, on 26 April 1974, the witness disappeared on a short drive to Julio de Mesquita and was found *six days* later, over five hundred miles away, sitting on a hillside and soaking wet. Later investigation revealed that he had been abducted aboard a UFO and medically examined by blond-haired entities.

And the encounters continue. At Mirassol, only ten miles from Sao José do Rio Preto, a new twist was added on 18 June 1979, when a dark-skinned man was abducted by dark-skinned entities. This occurred at three a.m. while he was on guard duty at a factory. He claims he was taking a shower when a strange object descended on the patio and three small beings emerged. They paralysed him with beams emitted from boxes on their chests ahead. This had a blue light in the middle and other white lights. Fearful, the car driver leapt out and was then hit by a powerful beam of white light, in which he felt stifling heat. The object took off and flew away. Immediately stepping back into the car he discovered that his peculiar passenger had vanished, but had left the door open – and the wrenched-off door handle on the floor!

Driving around in the early hours of the morning on the outskirt roads of Bahia Blanca seems to be a good way to meet UFOs. It happened again to a truck driver, Dionisio Llanca, making the long overnight trip south to Patagonia. At around 1.15 a.m. on 28 October 1973, on the road south-west of the city, he had stopped at Villa Bordeu to change a faulty tyre when his nightmare began.

The road was lit by a brilliant yellow beam which turned blue. Then he noticed he could not stand up, but could turn around on his knees to see a disc-like craft over nearby trees . . . and three strange entities standing close by, as if watching him work on the wheel. Two were male, one female. The men had blond hair and sloping eyes, speaking in strange high-pitched squeaks. One put a small implement to the truck driver's finger and painlessly extracted some blood, after which he lost consciousness. He recovered almost two hours later some miles away, with no memory of who he was – let alone how he got there. Llanca was taken to Bahia Blanca's main hospital. Police later found his truck jacked up, with the wheel still unchanged, just where he had left it.

In hospital, Llanca's memory returned. He was subjected to investigation by many doctors and psychiatrists, including hypnotic regression and truth drugs. He could only recall a little of what occurred inside the UFO, where he believed he was taken. Later, one of the doctors, Eladio Santos, summarized the views of the research team, saying,

We possess no means of proving that Llanca was not inside a flying object, nor do we possess a technique capable of proving that he was . . . [but] he always told the same story . . . that he was inside a flying saucer with two tall men and a woman with long red hair . . . They promised to return . . .

However, if cruising the streets at night is none too wise, it is the Sierra de la Ventana, a mountain range some fifty miles north-east of the city, and notably to the town of Tres Arroyos at its southern edge, where we must go to find the region which has provoked more sightings than anywhere else.

On 14 October 1972, at 4 a.m., climbers on the Tres Picos observed a strange dark cloud that rotated with flashing lights.

On 28 November 1972, the TV set failed in the home of a retired airline pilot. A being with a blue suit materialized in his armchair and imitated everything the witness did before declining a glass of water. Eventually the being went into the yard, looked at the sky, pressed a few buttons on a belt and vanished. Several similar cases to this have occurred around the world.

However, the most amazing event of all at Tres Arroyos took place on 30 December 1972, and involved an uneducated gaucho, aged seventy-three, and his pet cat.

Late one night his radio failed and a loud humming noise filled the air above his remote shack. Looking up he saw a powerful light beaming down, which emerged from a wheellike object; on the underside tubes churned out sparks. A cabin with windows in the middle contained a strange figure, wearing a suit made up of rolled material. The being stared down at him as the object tilted on to its edge. Then, after a few seconds, a huge flash of light shot out and hit the cat, which fled. The gaucho was himself temporarily blinded by this. Meanwhile, the humming noise increased in intensity and the UFO flew over some trees leaving the smell of sulphur.

The cat vanished for several days and returned with its skin singed and its personality altered to total shyness. The gaucho also developed headaches, nausea and blisters on his skin. Then clumps of his hair fell out. After he recovered, he noticed that new teeth were growing through his gums – which, given his age, was hardly normal.

Much of this was verified by investigation teams, as was the severe burning damage to the tops of the trees over which the object hovered. But strangest of all was that this man who could hardly read and write suddenly developed a fascination for subjects like philosophy and science.

He later admitted that the UFO had returned in February 1973 and an entity from this had told him many things; his recollection included a complex medical discussion which gave an alleged cure for cancer. The language is in many ways obscure and the description of this cure offers only brief snatches of lucidity.

Certainly a visit to this town or the foothills of the mountains to its north could be a good base for a skywatch.

Puerto Rico

This small island between Florida in the north and Venezuela in the south is famous for its magical rituals and association with Voodooism. But it also has a healthy tradition of UFO events. Indeed, it has had some of the most aggressive and unnerving close-encounter cases ever recorded.

In October 1973, a wave of activity focused on the area around the capital San Juan. Numerous rotating lights were seen, some by police officers, and through telescopes. On 28 October, at Rio Pedras, a vivid glow in the sky emitted rays and appeared to probe people on the ground. It made off across the Fuentes Fluviales electricity-generating station – maintaining the tradition of UFO association with such places.

In early 1975, the most sinister phase began on the north-west corner of the island around Aguadilla. This involved the discovery of numerous animals killed under strange circumstances. Often there was little sign of injury and there was never any blood. Although suspicion immediately linked them with ancient island rituals, the mutilation phenomenon has been a widespread part of the UFO mystery since the 1960s, when cattle in the mid-western states of America were found in the same bizarre circumstances. Some researchers allege that aliens had been using advanced surgical techniques to extract DNA samples for their ongoing medical experiments.

As in America, in Puerto Rico the UFO phenomenon was soon to be linked with the animal deaths. In the midst of the killings, UFOs made regular appearances at Moca. For example, on 12 March, a spinning mass of lights was seen, and on 6 April, there was a wave of activity. This culminated in a sighting reported live over his radio show by DJ Willie Lopez who was watching a yellow saucer in the sky and had also seen a luminous figure from his station at Miramar. Soon after this, mysterious power failures hit the island.

Possibly the oddest of all the disturbing encounters took place at San German on 28 April 1975, at 3-30 a.m. A bright object appeared over the outside toilet of a home and beamed flashes of powerful light downward. As this happened the lavatory exploded into flames. There was a series of high pitched noises and the UFO disappeared.

In 1977 the aliens began to show themselves in person. On 12 July, at Quebradillo, a grotesque figure of short stature and with large pointed ears appeared near a house, wearing a driver's uniform. After being disturbed it glided into the air and flew away over trees to the utter amazement of the watching farmer.

The encounters have continued to escalate ever since and by 1980 had reached the point where a direct link was suggested between the animal mutilations and the small humanoid creatures.

On 3 March, at 3-30 a.m., a group of five beings were seen by a family at Rio Pedras after being disturbed by their barking dogs. Two were five-feet tall, but the others were only about three feet in height. They again had large pointed ears and wore diving suits. They moved around by floating just above the ground and seemed interested in chickens kept in pens within the yard, moving metal plating to try to get at them. At the same time nearby, other witnesses saw a landed bell-shaped object and several beings who floated up inside this. One was tall but most were smaller. They believe one of the entities was female.

If you visit this island and intend to try skywatching, the northern coast offers the best options. There are local legends that UFOs appear from under the water in the Puerto Rico Trench where the sea depth plunges dramatically just a few miles offshore. It should offer one of the more pleasant locations for UFO observation – and if you don't spot anything, then at least you can sunbathe!

Asia

Japan's Far North

Japan is a series of islands teeming with people but covered by geophysical activity – as the many violent earthquakes frequently demonstrate. This is exactly the sort of place where researchers would expect to find plenty of UFOs and they would be right. Indeed, there are reports of strange glows appearing in the sky immediately prior to the onset of earth tremors.

Possibly the most active location is on the northernmost island of Hokkaido, some five hundred miles north of Tokyo.

One of the most fascinating encounters was at Tomakomai, on the coast to the south of the mountain range that dominates the centre of the island. In July 1973, a man working on night patrol at a wood yard spotted a strange orange light in the sky, which spiralled downwards and then hovered over the bay. When only a few feet above the water a tube emerged from the mass of light and as it touched the sea it started to glow. To the witness's amazement it then sucked up water into the tube!

After a few minutes this stopped and the light grew dimmer, turning more white as the object rose upwards and headed inland towards the frightened security guard. The land surrounding him was lit up as bright as day, as the UFO drifted overhead. He could now see that it was a large drum-shaped craft with windows, behind which he saw shadowy figures. There were also several other glowing lights which had appeared in the sky nearby and these were pulled inside the larger craft, before it flew away at speed.

On 9 May 1982, a photograph was taken a little north of here at Asahikawa. The hatlike object with a dome appeared in broad daylight in the vicinity of the Taisetsuzan National Park, whose mountain backdrop forms an ideal setting for skywatching in this region.

However, possibly the best place for photography is on Japan's main island, Honshu, to the south between Osaka and Hiroshima.

A peculiar close encounter occurred in the Saitama Province on 3 October 1978, when a man drove to the top of a mountain to enter into long-range radio contact with his brother across several hundred miles. However, he came into contact with something else altogether.

A beam of light shone on to the car and struck his young daughter, who was resting on the back seat. She became covered in an orange glow. All electrical power faded from the vehicle and then a small creature with large ears appeared at the window as if attempting communication. The horrified witness saw a series of images flash through his mind before the car's power suddenly returned, and he fled the scene without even looking back to see how his daughter was. Aside from some minor physical effects, such as a headache, both witnesses did thankfully recover.

A mountain peak with a good open view just off the coast of Japan may also be one of the finest vantage points for seeking out UFOs, but as you can see it does have a few hazards to bear in mind.

The Malaysian Peninsula

This peninsula stretches into the South China Sea, south of Thailand, and has generated a unique series of UFO encounters with a flavour of their own. When heavily stationed with British soldiers, soon after the Second World War, there was already much activity. An entire platoon encountered an object shaped like a disc with a dome on top and emitting a high-pitched noise. This was at Port Dickson and the morse code equipment carried by the troop stopped working whilst the UFO passed

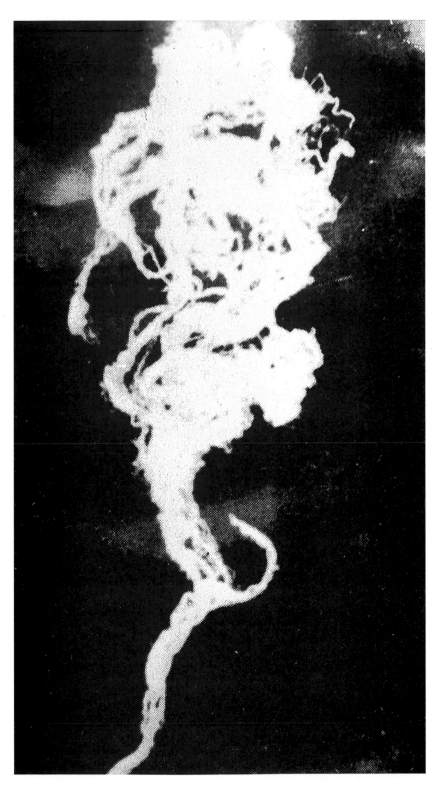

A peculiarity of many UFO sightings in the 1950s was the alleged fall of a fine filament like material, which dropped from passing objects in a manner not unlike snow. More recent cases have included strange deposits being found on cars after they were enveloped by UFOs. The material was called 'angel hair', and some argued it was simply spider's web. This angel hair fell after a UFO sighting in Hokkaido, Japan in April 1957.

A UFO being chased by a jet plane over Hya Kuri base, Japan in October 1975? Or is it merely a processing blemish that accidentally turned up on a photograph of the aircraft? The dispute rages. You be the judge.

over – making this one of the oddest reports of the well-known electrical interference effect.

However, by far the majority of UFO activity seems to happen a little further north in the region known as Pinang, separating the west-central coast from the tiny island of Pinang itself. This includes much of the peculiar UFO type for which the region is noted – sightings of absolutely tiny entities, no more than a few inches in height!

A wave of such events took place in August 1970. Aside from the entities almost unprecedented size, which makes them more like fairies than UFO occupants, their description is similar to that of many of the other UFO occupants encountered around the world, outside the USA and Europe.

At Bukit Mertajan, for example, a three-inch-tall creature was encountered – complete with a tiny UFO. The being wore a typical one-piece suit and also had the commonly reported large ears. Oddly, most of the witnesses during this unusual wave were young children – leading to much suspicion about hoaxing. However, at least some of the cases seemed genuine. One boy was the son of a police officer and claimed the entity fired a small gun at him. His hand had to be treated for a minor injury.

Many of the inhabitants seemed to associate the small beings with local folklore rather than UFOs and excellent research into these cases has been carried out by island vet Ahmed Jamaludin. In 1976, for instance, one of the mini-aliens was reported right beside an airbase at Kuantan!

Just inland from Pinang is a range of mountains that stretches across the peninsula towards Terengganu. Here there has also been much activity. This is a good spot for an expansive view of the surroundings – although the island of Pinang itself might be more attractive.

In this hinterland at Kulim, in May 1979, a UFO with only about a two-foot diameter was seen flying

One of the many UFO photographs taken in Japan. This one shows an object over Kaizuka in 1958.

On 27 May 1968, a UFO
was seen by many people
in Port Klang and Kuala
Lumpur, Malaysia as it flew
towards the mountains in
the centre of the peninsula.
This photograph shows the
small saucerlike object.

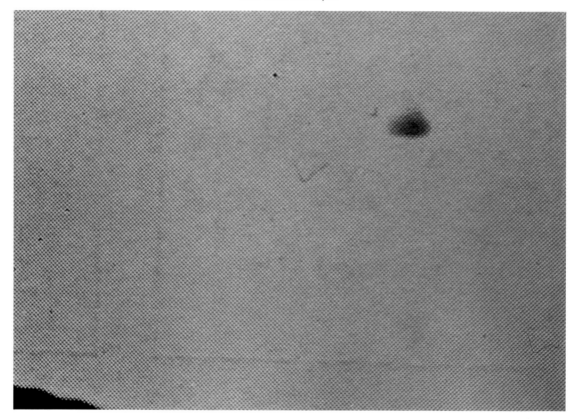

over some cows. It had three legs, which emerged from the main body as it proceeded to land. One of the witnesses attempted to touch the object but was promptly struck by a beam of light that shot out and temporarily blinded him. The cattle became so agitated they tried to break free of their tethers and escape.

On 8 June 1980 at Port Klang another destructive act was reported. A bright luminous ball that rotated and gave off various colours appeared above an oil refinery and seemed to shoot a beam of light straight at the complex, according to eye-wit-

nesses. The beam missed, but hit a house nearby, which erupted into flames, destroying several properties.

It has been noted that in less-developed nations UFOs tend to react in a much more aggressive manner when approached. This might make sky-watching difficult – although the special nature of Malaysian reports may well compensate. There has also been much activity of a not dissimilar nature just across the Indonesian Sea on the volcanic islands of Sumatra and Java. The adjacent island of Bali is a perfect spot to skywatch.

Australasia

The island continent of Australia is a wonderful place to look for UFOs. It has one of the lowest population densities in the world – with a vast interior that is almost uninhabited and all the major pockets of population spread in an arc around the south-eastern coasts. Yet it has a higher concentration of active UFO 'window areas' than anywhere else.

The Nullarbor Region

This may well be the most difficult area in which to plan a skywatch. It is a vast plain bordered on the south by the ocean and on the north by scrub that leads toward thousands of miles of seemingly endless desert. If you lose your way off the Eyre Highway which stretches as an incredible ribbon to form the main link between Perth and the bulk of the nation far to the east, then you could be in real trouble.

However, the several-day drive between Perth and Adelaide – or the rather more relaxing train journey which follows a parallel route (across the longest stretch of straight track ever built) – represents a challenge and an adventure for the hardy. It has the added bonus that you are passing through UFO territory.

So remote is the Nullarbor that the British exploded nuclear bombs around Maralinga in the 1950s – without, some claim, much concern about the consequences. The local Aboriginees are still most aggrieved, with due cause. There followed an amazing sighting during early November 1957, after a series of tests had ended. A man who is now a Home Office photographer, was present when he and colleagues saw a UFO appear right on top of the bomb site. He says it sat there tilted at an angle, 'perched like a king on his throne'.

The disc was clearly made out of silver metal and they could even see plates and windows in the side.

The object remained stationary for fifteen minutes as dusk fell across the Nullarbor and then it simply shot into the air without making any sound and disappeared.

The witness is a deeply committed Christian who says he would swear on a Bible that this event took place. Indeed it is thought by some to be one of the most important in the history of UFOs. Recall that on the night of the 2 and 3 November 1957 (quite conceivably the same day and at most a few days after Maralinga) the extraordinary series of vehicle stoppages took place at Levelland in Texas. That incident ended with the sighting of a UFO seen just west of here in New Mexico. That was a disc tilted at the same angle as the one at Maralinga. It hovered literally right above the site where, in July 1945, the world's first atomic weapon was detonated. Later that very day, the USSR launched Laika the dog into orbit – the first living thing from the earth to reach outer space.

Do we see an incredible sequence of happenings at this momentous time? Just as our world first enters space, two UFOs hover above nuclear test sites separated by half the planet – those where the very first and the most recent detonations had taken place. At the same time came a demonstration of how UFOs can seemingly override all electrical power on a scale never repeated. Coincidence? Or an attempt to tell us something?

On 4 February 1973, the Eyre Highway provoked one of its stranger encounters when a nurse and her boyfriend were driving towards Kimba in South Australia. They observed an orange rectangular glow in a field beside the road which seemed to contain a large white figure of humanoid appearance. The image resembled a person standing in a non-existent doorway. The couple accelerated past, but did look back to see that the glow now seemed to extend right across the road.

Excellent investigation by UFO Research Australia was able to confirm this experience. It was

A UFO seen in the sky at Mareeba, in the hinterland west of Cairns. It was reputedly taken in October 1972 by T. Nieuwenhuis, when he was trying to photograph star trails. He had left the camera pointing at the sky with the shutter open and did not see the UFOs that were recorded.

reported to police, who also went back to the location with the frightened witnesses that same night. It was a long journey back, but because of their obvious sincerity, the police were willing. Two other vehicles were on the road at the same time – a car and a truck driven by a man from Ceduna.

Both were traced and both report seeing something similar in the field. Despite its peculiar nature, an almost identical case occurred around the same time near Sheffield in Britain amidst the Pennine window.

However, the most famous of all Eyre Highway encounters made headlines in nearly every country, because by chance it occurred during the Australian Bi-Centennial celebrations on 21 January 1988.

A family were making their first epic car journey across the Nullarbor – eastwards from Perth to pay a surprise visit to relatives. In the early hours before dawn they had reached Mundrabilla, approaching the West Australia-South Australia state border. Here they saw an unusual light in the sky ahead and there followed a terrifying ordeal.

They claim that the car was 'attacked' by the light, which resembled an oval egg in an egg-cup base. At one point they even felt it sucked them up off the road and their tyre burst as they fell back down. The car slewed off the edge into scrub and they hid in the bush until the object was gone. When outside they heard a humming noise coming from the glowing shape.

Upon arrival at Mundrabilla the shaken family told their story. The car had four small dents in the roof and there was some evidence of a fine ash inside which smelt like bakelite. They eventually carried on with their journey, and reported the matter to police in Ceduna. After that their case became a media event and rival UFO groups and sceptics vied for an explanation.

One group claimed they analysed the dust and found strange materials in it, hinting at an artificial origin. The police forensic study disagreed, as did a report by the UFO Research Australia team. Both said the powder was worn brake lining. A truck driver who passed the scene did confirm the story and did see a distant light. Indeed a few people on the highway that night told of being hit by a sudden blast that rocked their vehicles, or of seeing lights in the sky. From this evidence some scientists suggested an unusual mirage effect coupled with an electrical storm or tornado. This might have been what was encountered. The case remains controversial from a number of respects, but is still considered most intriguing.

Such was the furore after this encounter that a sign was even erected on this highway to warn of the world's most unusual road hazard – UFOs!

The Bass Straits

This shallow region of sea at the extreme southern edge of the continent is bordered by Adelaide, Melbourne, and the island of Tasmania – forming a triangle as infamous as the mythical one off the shores of Bermuda. There have been many fateful reports of odd goings-on – the most controversial of which occurred in October 1978 amidst a huge wave of strange lights that were seen in the sky.

At 6.19 p.m. on 21 October, a young pilot named Frederick Valentich took off from Melbourne to fly to King Island – midway across the straits on the way to Tasmania. An hour later he was the subject of a tragic mystery which has never been resolved. Valentich never landed at the island. In fact, neither he nor his Cessna aircraft were ever seen again, after reporting over the radio that he was being shadowed by a strange formation of lights. The entire close encounter was recorded by the air-traffic control, followed by peculiar metallic noises and then silence. The accident enquiry never discovered what happened.

Over the years there have been many attempts to solve the mystery and a number of puzzles. For example, Valentich was interested in UFOs and even seems to have taken a scrapbook of UFO press cuttings with him. Some speculate that he set up the UFO sighting as a cover for some other activity or an escape to a new identity, but such ideas have never been justified. Most who knew him seem to believe he really did have a fateful close encounter with an unknown object.

The coastal area from which he departed is one with a long record of UFO activity. It was also the hub of a crop-circle mystery, long before such patterns reached southern England.

At Wokurna, to the south-east of Adelaide, a strange mark a few feet in diameter appeared in a wheat field in early December 1973. Investigation was conducted by Peter Horne and Stephen Bolton of the UFO Research Australia team. From their account, and photographs of what were popularly known as 'saucer nests', it is evident that this phenomenon was a smaller version of what was later to cause a stir 10,000 miles away. Theories ranged from rotating wind to kangaroos – which obviously were not behind the British circles!

Seven swirled circles (up to fourteen feet in diameter) appeared nearby at Bordertown in a field of oats and were investigated by Keith Basterfield. Indeed, the whole area seems to have regularly produced them. This is proof that crop circles are not a new phenomenon, nor one confined to Britain.

Links with UFOs also exist. In the Mallee wheat belt of Victoria, west of Melbourne (an extension of

Pilot Frederick Valentich, who vanished on a flight between Melbourne and King Island in the Bass Straits in October 1978. This was amidst a UFO wave in the area and immediately after reporting a close encounter over the radio that he said occurred between his Cessna and a UFO.

the Bordertown and Wokurna area), a remarkable series of circles – some only a few inches in diameter, others many feet wide – appeared on land owned by the Jolly's in early December 1989. In fact, as many as ninety of them were found in all – which would challenge any site in Britain. Although it was extensively reported in the media, the Jolly's told me something they had not publicly reported, because they did not think it would be understood. During the period of hot, stable weather when it

seems these circles formed, a number of strange darting and flashing lights were seen in the sky above the fields. They had similarities with lightning, but were most peculiar. The farmers have also heard screaming noises in the night – like the sound of a jet engine and shrill insects or whistles.

Staking out the wheat belt on the South Australia-Victoria state border region in late November and early December of any year looks to be an excellent idea for hopeful skywatchers. However, if it is real

UFOs you are looking for, make the short hop across the Bass Straits to the island of Tasmania – hosting the best concentration of close-encounter activity in the country. The north of the island, especially around Launceston, is a good place to start. There are plenty of hills for good visibility and some nice fishing lakes to camp by.

There have been numerous waves and a number of spectacular cases. On 26 February 1975, two people who were camped for fishing by Lake Sorell had a close view of a UFO that plunged out of cloud and hovered above the lake with a brilliant sweeping beam shining on to the surface, and lighting up the area like day. Before it disappeared in a flash it switched off the beam, leaving an eerie white glow floating in the air for some time.

But the most common types of event in Tasmania seem to be those which involve interference with car engines. There are more cases from this area than anywhere else in the world.

On 20 August 1979, near Waratah, a retired police officer found her car soaked in a green glow which was coming from a light on the road behind. She put her foot on the pedal but the car slowed, rather than accelerated. In addition the brake failed to stop the car when applied. It was as if it was held in a grip by the UFO. After some minutes, the

One of the earliest-ever crop circles at Wokurna, in a region where many such marks continue to appear. This was part of a major investigation by the UFO Research Australia team in December 1972. Some said kangaroos were responsible for these 'saucer nests', but there were many similarities with modern-day crop circles. Peter Horne's photographs may yet be of great value to those researching crop circles.

light disappeared and the car returned to normal, but the dashboard clock and the woman's wrist-watch had stopped. Both later worked without repair.

Frightening cases where car engines and lights fail completely have also continued, while in the rest of the world they are now quite rare.

On 14 December 1987, a dealer delivering a car some twenty miles south of Launceston observed odd lights and then a grey egg-shape which landed on the road ahead. On the underside of this object were bright lights which hurt the eyes to look at. The danger of collision was averted because both the engine and lights on the shiny Mercedes failed and instinctively the driver hit the brakes and slowed the car to a halt.

In absolute terror he jumped out to hide behind a tree, just in time to watch the UFO start to drag his stalled and unoccupied car thirty feet along the road, as if it were being pulled by a giant magnet. Skid marks were left on the road surface and bitumen melted off in places, before the car stopped dead. The car dealer was violently ill as he looked on, possibly from shock.

A diesel-powered truck came down the road a few minutes later and reached the scene just as the UFO took off skyward at great speed. Its lights failed but the engine continued to operate – something that has happened before with diesel-powered vehicles. This is obviously a key to the energy forces that are involved in close encounters.

It may possibly be good advice, if driving around the roads of northern Tasmania looking for UFOs, that if you want to keep control of the situation, drive a car *without* a normal ignition system.

The Kempsey Region

This is a rural area of the MacLeay River valley that cuts through the New England range of mountains in northern New South Wales. It is about 250 miles from Sydney and has long been thought of as a UFO 'window'.

This was notably true after a series of lights in the sky appeared here in early April 1971, and ending with the remarkable claims of an Aboriginee.

Whilst standing by the sink in his kitchen he says that a force sucked him through the glass – despite an iron bar blocking the way. He recovered consciousness, with minor cuts and bruises and without any idea how this could have happened.

But that was just the start. Later that month, an orange light was frequently seen in the area between the town and the coast. At Crescent Head on 17 April, two fishermen watched it hover over the sea. Despite being twice as large as the moon it left no reflection on the water.

The UFO at Kempsey, New South Wales in July 1975. The region is famous for its UFO sightings, but opinion amongst UFO investigators is divided as to whether this is the UFO that moved across the sky or a planet photographed by accident as it was setting near the horizon.

At Colombatti on 24 April, a manta-ray shape with beams of light coming from the front seemed to land on a farm. A teacher saw it at the same time from a hill near Kempsey, saying it was 'so beautiful it was stunning'.

Then, on 10 May, at Willi Willi, the sky turned flaming red and an object plunged out of clouds giving a perfect view to those underneath. It appeared to be a metallic dome with rilles along the edge. As it moved away the sky returned to its normal steely grey. Investigations at the Colombatti farm revealed no evidence of a landing but a fascinating history of strange activity which continued into 1972. In January on several occasions the barn began to shake violently in the middle of the night. On 16 January one of these attacks coincided with the sighting of another light over the farm.

On 21 July 1975, Kempsey generated its most famous encounter when a brilliant light was seen travelling after dusk, faster than any aircraft and moving towards the west. It then appeared to hover low on the horizon and changed colour above the distant hills. A series of photographs was taken over the next fifteen minutes, using fast-rated film adapted for the dark. These depict the UFO dropping downward, as if 'landing' behind the hills, before a telephoto lens could be fitted.

Investigator Keith Basterfield later announced that computer read-outs showed that the object must have been the then brilliant planet Venus, or 'there should have been two bright light sources in the picture'. Whilst acknowledging this problem, original investigator Bill Chalker notes that the witnesses say the object moved at speed across a wide arc of sky before hovering. Venus could not do this. Perhaps the planet chanced to be in the sky near where the UFO had vanished and so was easily mistaken as a result.

Later that year a truck driver on the road to Armidale observed strange things twice, including another object that seemed to land in a field. Just outside Armidale some years later, a farmer underwent a very strange experience in which what appeared to be an invisible force field prevented him or his vehicle from escaping the property. It was as if a bell-jar had been placed over the farm, producing unseen walls that resisted all attempts to exit the area.

However, the strangest vehicle interference effect was at Nemingha, to the west of Kempsey and just outside of Tamworth. This was at 5.45 a.m. on the morning of 22 March 1976, and involved a family returning home from holiday with a caravan in tow. They stopped at a crossroads to try to decide the best route to travel and saw an approaching car. Their intention was to ask the driver for advice but events rapidly overtook them.

A yellow-green light came down from the sky and enveloped the other car, which immediately seemed to lose control and swerve on to the wrong side of the road. By now it was covered by a white misty glow. It then came to a halt and had apparently lost all power from both its engine and lights.

The white mist surrounded the car for a couple of minutes and then just vanished, leaving the terrified woman driver to get out of her stricken vehicle, desperately trying to get rid of some of the thick white powder that had been deposited all over the bodywork and windscreen. As she was doing this

her car headlights came back on spontaneously and she quickly drove away, casting the cloth on to the roadside before doing so. To everyone's amazement this cloth – covered in the white deposit – burst into flames.

Evidently, this country region of New South Wales has some very intriguing natural phenomena associated with it.

The Reef and Rainforest Region

Far North Queensland on the north-easterly tip of Australia is one of the most fascinating places to visit. Its sub-tropical climate brings tourists to the

small town of Cairns to see where the reef meets the rainforest. The Great Barrier Reef stretches along the coast with its breathtaking submerged islands of living coral set in a warm ocean. On the coast this almost touches the teaming rainforest tumbling into the sea.

Aside from this natural beauty it is also full of tales of both UFOlogy and crop circles. Indeed, it is the home of the crop-circle mystery.

The first 'saucer nests' appeared in early 1966 in the Tully rainforest area south of Cairns. A thirty-foot diameter patch of swirled and flattened reeds was discovered floating on a shallow swampy area. The edge of the swirled area was standing completely straight. Aside from its unusual location, the nest was in all respects exactly like the crop circles later to appear in South Australian cereal fields, and

Far North Queensland is another UFO-haunted region, dominated by the beauty of the Great Barrier Reef in the warm Coral Sea.

UFO sightings have occurred over the outer reef, shallow islands of just-submerged coral, as well as inland in the bush.

much later still to take the world by storm when they sprang up in southern England wheat fields.

After publicity and numerous search parties into the fairly impenetrable area, several more similar nests were discovered – although rather smaller than the original. There was speculation that the UFO – which residents deemed responsible – had come north from Mackay.

Certainly in the mountains near here there was an interesting sighting just after midnight on 24 May 1965. People at a retreat hotel observed a large

Although many assumed the circle mystery began in 1980 (indeed some well-known circle writers even seem unaware of that starting date!), UFO researchers have been aware of older cases, such as that at Tully in 1966. A search for historical anecdotes has traced some cases, including a woodcut about mown circles left by the devil at Hertfordshire in August 1678.

THE MOWING-DEVIL:
OR, STRANGE NEWS OUT OF
HARTFORD-SHIRE.

Being a True Relation of a Farmer, who Bargaining with a Poor Mower, about the Cutting down Three Half Acres of Oats: upon the Mower's asking too much, the Farmer swore *That the Devil should Mow it rather than He.* And so it fell out, that very Night, the Crop of Oat shew'd as if it had been all of a Flame; but next Morning appear'd so neatly mow'd by the Devil or some Infernal Spirit, that no Mortal Man was able to do the like.

Also, How the said Oats ly now in the Field, and the Owner has not Power to fetch them away.

Licensed, August 22nd, 1678.

disc that hovered over some trees with a massive bank of lights shining down. It appeared very close to the ground but eventually left north-eastward. One witness was a retired pilot and a justice of the peace. The police investigated and found singed tops to the trees and a perfect circle on the ground where the grass had been laid flat.

Which exactly were the first 'nests' is open to a deal of confusion. Some UFO records state clearly that they appeared as early as May 1965, but these seem to be confused with the events of 19 January 1966, when banana-grower George Pedley found one on the Horseshoe Lagoon on a neighbour's cane farm at Euramo near Tully. The event is significant because Pedley may have seen the circle form.

The farmer was on his tractor when the engine began to fail and a hissing noise brought his attention to the swampland just in front of him. Rising out of here was a grey oval mass. The water was still rotating in an anti-clockwise circle as the object

The famous 'crop circle' at Euramo near Tully, which formed in a lagoon in January 1966 after an oval mass rose skyward. The mat of reeds have been torn from the bottom and were floating in a swirled pattern on the surface. Self-confessed crop-circle hoaxers Doug Bower and Dave Chorley in September 1991 credited this case with giving them the idea to fake circles in English cereal fields years later.

with a vaporous form climbed upwards and disappeared. It left behind a smell of sulphur and a typical nest swirled into the reed bed and floating on the water surface. The reeds were brown and dead but had been alive the night before. Some think that the UFO which rose from the water might have arrived at around five-thirty a.m., some hours earlier, because the landowner's dog went 'crazy' at this time and reportedly rushed towards the lagoon.

Three days later, a little further north at Cooktown, the local police sergeant had a weird experience when he saw several large bubbles of about three feet in diameter floating on the road surface ahead. He drove over them without ill-effect and they disappeared.

Also around the time when these 'nests' were discovered in the Tully area came an alleged sighting above the outer barrier reefs. It was on 28 May 1965, and an Ansett aircraft was directly involved.

At 3.25 a.m. the pilot of the flight north from Brisbane reported seeing a flattened sphere in the sky, which dogged the DC-6 for several minutes as it flew over the reefs off-shore from Tully and Cairns. The pilot took several pictures of the object before it finally shot away.

He was immediately informed over the radio to leave the film unprocessed until he flew back to Canberra. Upon his arrival there military authorities took the roll and also the ground-to-air recordings from the airport-control tower at Townsville.

This claim has been strongly denied by the Australian government.

So many nests continued to appear near Tully (and indeed still do today) that an automatic movie camera was set up at the site. This would start to film if something in the swamp was to move. The set-up allegedly triggered one night in early 1968 but the film reputedly vanished on its way from Tully to the Kodak laboratories.

Bill Chalker, who investigated many of Australia's best cases, swam in Horseshoe Lagoon to follow up the saucer nest stories. He has a piece of advice for anyone visiting the area in the hope of seeing something unusual: the water is infested with deadly Taipan snakes. 'I only found out after I stepped out,' he said.

But you have been warned!

Europe

It would be impossible to cover all window areas on this continent as there are many. The most recent comes in an area traditionally devoid of sightings – eastern Belgium. Perhaps because of this, the arrival of a major wave here generated massive publicity, which in turn led to more reports. In nations where UFOs are widely discussed such a cycle has less impact.

Belgium

In fact, the sightings in Belgium are remarkably consistent. They began in November 1989 at Eupen and most of the hundreds that followed were in country around Namur and Liège, towards the German border. Almost all were of huge triangular objects with bright lights at each apex; which is in fact a common UFO type (see page 132). The reports came in short bursts and then there was a lengthy lull, as in all waves. By early 1991 they

▲ Not all active window areas in Europe are easy to visit. This is the site of an alleged series of events deep in the sub-continent of the former USSR, near a remote mountain range at Dalnegorsk. A strange ball of light reputedly hit the hill slopes in 1986 and exploded, creating much local damage. Some argue that it may have been a small comet or particle of anti-matter, and it has similarities with another famous Soviet explosion in Siberia many years before.

▶ The most recent European wave has centred on Belgium between 1989 and 1991 and featured a triangle of lights or a triangular object such as this. But the many sightings have not resolved the question of what the UFO may be.

were occurring only sporadically. However, there had been major government interest. Indeed, in March 1990 a remarkable experiment took place.

The local UFO group, SOBEPS (a Belgian study group into aerial phenomena), who had documented the high-calibre sightings from police officers, scientists and other reputable witnesses entered a liaison with the Belgian Air Force involving radar tracking and jets that were mobilized to pursue any UFOs reported to the group. It paid off and an unprecedented mid-air encounter with film of the airborne radar chase was released – although some researchers felt that some sort of optical mirage effect might have been what was involved in this case.

Undoubtedly, many of the Belgian triangles were misperceptions of stars or aircraft. But there does appear to have been a genuine phenomenon amidst all of this. Opinion is divided between those who say it was a real UFO and those who suspect it must have been American Stealth aircraft on secret tests. The American government strongly deny this and have even released Intelligence documents under freedom-of-information powers to show their puzzlement at the Belgian sightings. Eastern Belgium is still a good bet for a skywatch.

The Balearics, Spain

These romantic islands off the east-central Spanish coast remain one of the most popular tourist spots in Europe – in particular, the heavily frequented Majorca. However, the smaller and more laid-back island of Ibiza is traditionally a classic UFO window.

The Mediterranean Sea around the islands has provoked several startling mid-air UFO encounters recently. On 11 November 1979, a jet on a holiday flight from Majorca to Tenerife hit trouble after passing over Ibiza. Seconds after an attempted warning from Barcelona radar control (who were tracking the object but were thwarted by a radio-interference effect), two red lights swooped towards the TAE Airlines jet. They played tag with the aircraft for several minutes. After ordering the passengers to put on their seatbelts, serving them dinner, but not telling them about the UFO, Captain

Tejada made the decision to divert to the nearest airport – which was Valencia. They made a safe landing here and the passengers were rapidly sent to a hotel for the night without explanation, while the plane was checked over for faults. Thankfully there were none.

Several ground radars which had tracked the object, including military defence, showed that the UFO dropped vertically through twelve thousand feet in just thirty seconds – hence the aborted warning to the TAE plane. As soon as the passenger aircraft landed, several Mirage fighters were scrambled from a base at Albacete. One was similarly buzzed by the UFO and the other reputedly obtained film from its 'gun camera' which has never been released. After mounting an enquiry, the Spanish Transport Minister, Salvador Teran, said a few days later, 'It is clear that UFOs exist.'

Exactly one year to the day, there was a repeat performance when no less than *seven* aircraft (including one French and one British) had mid-air encounters north of the islands. A green soap bubble was engaged in a wide range of aerial activities which ended when it reportedly 'buzzed' the runway at Barcelona and flew off!

However, if your trip to the Baléarics has a high chance of being an eventful one you may well find the tranquillity of Ibiza rather deceptive when you get there. In particular, the hilly region in the hinterland behind San Antonio Abad has tales to tell.

There are several reports of a glowing orange ball of light which appears on the hill slopes. In one close encounter it was said to make a terrific *whoomph-whoomph* sound that was painful to the ears, suggesting a displacement of air pressure.

In addition, the wooded region around Santa Eulalia del Rio has produced a number of sightings of entities. In one case, a group of children observed a silvery metal figure and another in a flowing robe standing beside a tree. This was before noting a strange glowing light in the woods.

Some locals believe that there is a UFO base on the small rocky island of Formentera, situated off the southerly tip of Ibiza. Many lights have been seen in the vicinity by ships and tourists on the mainland. A trip out here might prove worthwhile to would-be skywatchers.

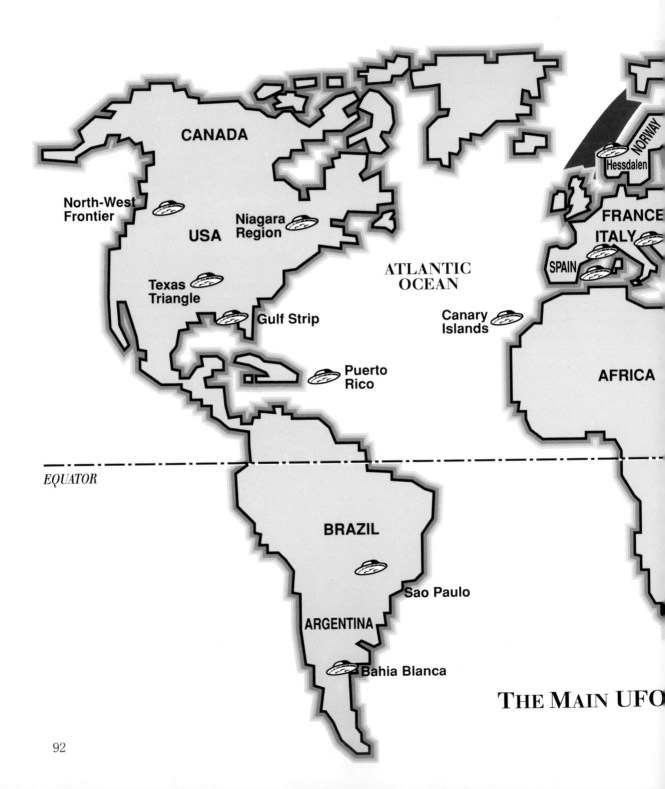

CANADA

North-West
Frontier

Niagara
Region

USA

Texas
Triangle

Gulf Strip

ATLANTIC
OCEAN

NORWAY

Hessdalen

FRANCE

ITALY

SPAIN

Canary
Islands

AFRICA

Puerto
Rico

EQUATOR

BRAZIL

Sao Paulo

ARGENTINA

Bahia Blanca

THE MAIN UFO

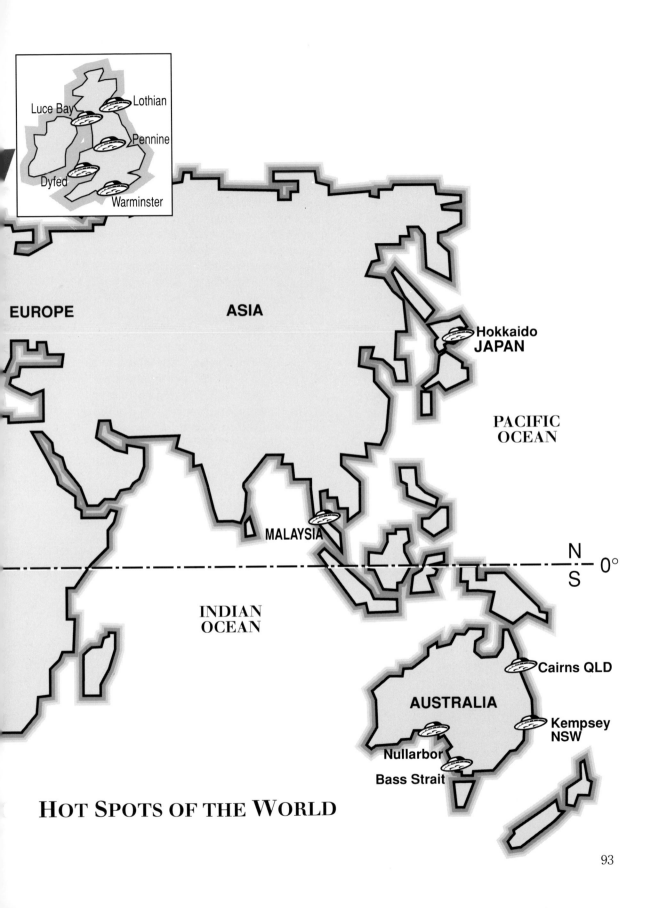

EUROPE

ASIA

Luce Bay
Lothian
Pennine
Dyfed
Warminster

Hokkaido
JAPAN

PACIFIC
OCEAN

MALAYSIA

N
S
0°

INDIAN
OCEAN

Cairns QLD

AUSTRALIA

Kempsey
NSW

Nullarbor

Bass Strait

HOT SPOTS OF THE WORLD

Pordenone, North-Eastern Italy

A strategic area to the north and east of Venice, this is another region with plenty of UFO activity. Little news has filtered out about an incident at the Istrana air base in November 1973. However, the story has similarities with the landing at RAF Bentwaters in England (see page 00), in that the observation was by security guards on the base perimeter, who reportedly saw a strange object on the ground and two small humanlike beings who were dressed in white coveralls. As if disturbed when spotted, they got into the object and it took off, but marks were later found on the ground where it was assumed that the UFO had landed. Intense secrecy enshrouded the incident.

This again was true of an encounter at nearby Aviano air base late on 1 July 1977. This was even more like the Bentwaters incidents three years later. An object, described by airmen and civilians as a disc with a platelike base, was seen to hover above the secure area at this major NATO unit. Coincident with this, all electrical power seems to have been lost in the area. There was also disturbance to local dogs, possibly connected with a high-pitched whistle the object gave off. It was on-base for some time before it departed towards the mountains. Another military cover-up allegedly resulted and a silly explanation (quite literally moonshine!) officially vented.

On 14 April 1985, a young couple drove into the mountain ski resort of Piancavallo in a heavy storm, with much snow on the road. But a curious yellow-green fog suddenly descended on to their car and they noticed that the snow had locally melted. Still puzzling at this, the car engine failed. As they were on a downward hill they were able to coast a little way and their headlights still functioned. Through these they picked out two strange creatures that just stepped out from bushes right in front of the car!

The entities were tall (over six feet) and had silvery suits on their bodies. Curiously, these were disproportionately *wide*. The couple raced into a nearby village and were driven home by friends.

When they later collected their stricken car with a tow truck, it started first time without problem.

At nearby San Quirino that night a witness saw a saucerlike object with a greenish-yellow dome on top. It dropped from the sky to a very low height, then started to move in a jerky manner before streaking away.

The dangers of these mountain roads were revealed by another case on 6 August 1987. Three men were driving from Barcis to Cimolais late at night when a red beam from the sky surrounded them and the car lost all power. They jumped out to find an oval object directly overhead with a beam pouring out and lighting up the area as bright as day. In panic they scrambled back into the car which now appeared to be working again. Meanwhile the light had vanished.

In a confused state the three men realized that they were now lost. In fact, they were some miles away from where they had been when they met the UFO – at San Danièle. They had no memory of how they got there and went to the local hospital where they were treated for shock, nausea and conjunctivitis, presumably because of the brilliance of the lightbeam.

As you have noted, many of the best skywatching locations where UFOs are so common are to be found in the foothills of mountains or hills. Even if the areas you choose are not part of a recognized UFO window, look for these geographical features – especially ones within a region with much earthquake activity (as in the case of Venice). Alternatively, seek hills where there are natural features that host hydro-electric plants or dams.

Provence, France

This region in the extreme south-east of France stretches eastward from Marseilles and inland towards the Alps. It has by far the most focused group of close-encounter activity in a country that has produced many important cases. It challenges Britain for the European record.

The classic landing with entities in the lavender fields of Valensole in 1965 has already been reported, but this by no means exhausts the situ-

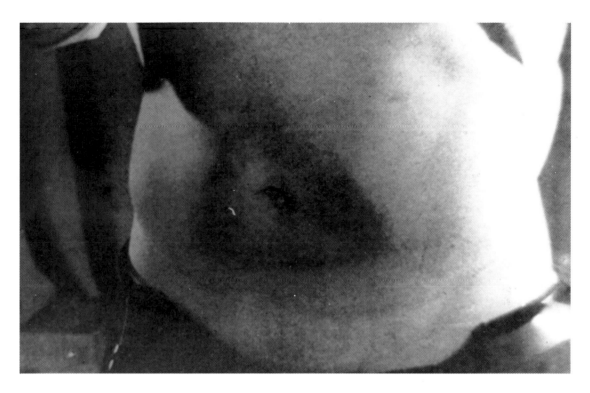

Dr 'X', the pseudonym given by researcher Aimé Michel to the highly respected scientist who was struck by a light beam from a UFO in his French valley home. Afterwards both he and his young son developed an identical red triangular blotch around their abdomen.

ation. Another very important case was investigated by Dr Jacques Vallée and is of particular significance because it involves an almost identical object performing in almost exactly the same way over a similar geographical location as one just two days earlier on a bridge over Loch Raven dam near Baltimore, Maryland, in America. The highly credible American case was not publicized when it happened and there is no conceivable way the witness to the subsequent French case could have known about it. To all intents and purposes the two events seem to involve the same object in some sort of on-going global surveillance operation.

The French case occurred on 28 October 1958, when a man was driving through a gorge west of Veynes and approaching an iron bridge over the Grand Beuch River. Ahead, over the rail tracks, was an object described as 'two plates glued together'. He drove right up to it and stood directly beneath the object. Sparks were emerging from the base. After being there just a couple of minutes the thing shot upwards to vanish in a split second, leaving a trail of fire and then a glow in the air which dissipated. His car was rocked by a violent blast of air as it did so.

Just about the only major differences reported in the Loch Raven case were that the car's electrical power failed and that when the UFO shot off the air displacement was heard by people in the surrounding area as a sonic boom or thunderclap. Vallée rightly suggested that these cases offered a 'challenge to science', as he called it in 1967. He is still endeavouring to respond to that challenge.

The remarkable 'Dr X' case investigated by Aimé Michel involved very similar shaped objects, which seemed to suck power from an electric storm that formed over the valley early in the morning of 2 November 1968.

The man insisted on anonymity owing to his status as a respected scientist but the extraordinary effects on himself and his fourteen-month-old child, bathed by light from the hovering UFOs, attest to its importance. An old war wound was cured overnight, as was a more minor injury from an axe that had just been incurred. More amazingly both the doctor and his son developed a red triangular mark around their abdomens. This recurred for several years, on both victims simultaneously, even when separated by many miles.

However, if you are looking to skywatch in this area, forsake the tourist attractions of the nearby Côte d'Azur or the pleasures of the high Alps and focus on the remarkable old town of Draguignan, about ten miles west of Cannes.

The name actually means 'dragon town', and a lot of what goes on there is said to be associated with Le Malmont (literally the 'evil mountain') to the north-west of the town. These names suggest that a rich history of strange forces may be linked with the area. It will probably not surprise you to learn that many major earth faults run through the area and the mountain itself – which some researchers believe is the reason for the natural energy forces that generate so many sightings.

Although lights and oval UFOs have appeared frequently around the town, perhaps the most important case of all took place at Trans-en-Provence, which is about a mile south-east of here. It occurred at dusk on 8 February 1981, when Monsieur Collini was working in his garden. Suddenly he heard a strange whistling sound and looked up in time to see a glowing disc falling on to the terraced slopes by his home. The object touched down briefly and then rose upwards. Rushing to the spot he saw that a circular impression and some indentations had been left where the object had landed. He immediately called the police, who, satisfied by his story and the markings notified GEPAN.

During the 1980s, GEPAN ('Study group into novel atmospheric phenomena') was unique, as an official group of scientists based at the space centre in Toulouse (the French equivalent of NASA). They had a government grant of good proportions to investigate UFO cases whenever the gendarmerie thought a report was significant enough to warrant scientific attention. Although no longer operational in the same form, and now rather more secretive than in the past, the GEPAN of 1981 was by far the best-funded UFO group in the world and published several limited circulation reports (including one on this case) that are of lasting value.

Whilst GEPAN got on with studying the physical after-effects of the case, a psychological laboratory was contracted to probe Monsieur Collini himself. They found his story completely reliable and consistent. More importantly, as Jean Velasco, the space engineer who then ran the project pointed out, there were internal and external consistencies between his story and the physical evidence.

Three independent laboratory tests of the soil and plants from the site were carried out. This revealed they had been heated and compressed and that the chlorophyll content of the leaves had been significantly reduced. You could plot the amount of effect at various distances from the centre of the landing zone. Such evidence clearly suggested that a radiating energy source – which decayed according to normal physical laws – was responsible for the damage. But they could only ascertain that it resembled a very intense electro-magnetic field – presumably the sort that in other cases can stop car engines.

There are some UFO experts who regard the Trans-en-Provence case as one of the most important ever studied.

If you plan to skywatch on Le Malmont there is a winding road that leads up towards the summit, and a small picnic area with a plaque at a viewing spot, shortly before this is reached. In daytime, it offers a splendid all-round view, but it is not the sort of drive to make in the dark. So make sure you ascend and descend in the light.

On 19 October 1973, a courting couple encountered an orange ball of light circled by a revolving halo as they climbed the mountain on their motorcycle. They left in a hurry but a group of four men whom they told about this on their arrival back in Draguignan decided to drive in two cars up the road towards the viewing area. They had a frightening encounter as a result, seeing both a strange light and several very tall figures in diver's suits. The four men fled the hill but one of the cars briefly lost motive power and nearly went out of control on the winding track. Luckily, electricity returned after a few seconds and they were able to escape.

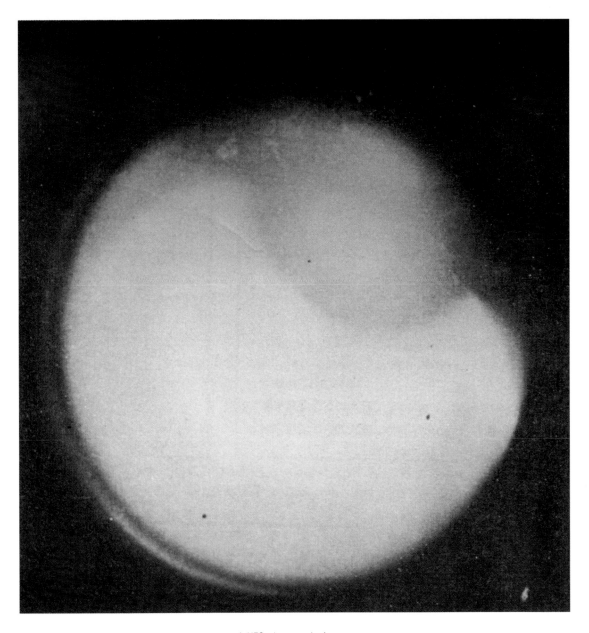

A UFO photographed at
Uzès near Nîmes, France in
November 1974. The object
was like a soap bubble and
a wall could be seen
through it. Strange blue
electric discharges were
noticed in the area several
times afterwards.

Scandinavia

The Hessdalen Valley, Norway

During the 1980s this remote valley in central Norway, some seventy miles south-east of Trondheim and not far south of the Arctic Circle, became the centre of the UFO universe. For here was the one place where you could go to see UFOs almost to order. The real problem was that it was very difficult to reach and even more difficult to stay there during the bitter winter months, when the sightings were at their peak and the temperature at a freezing *minus* thirty degrees centigrade.

The valley came to note in late 1981 when farmers in the small, scattered communities started to report lights in the sky. These were usually white or yellow-orange but were also occasionally blue. Mostly they were single blobs but sometimes they were in chains which seemed to many witnesses to suggest structured shapes. Some UFOlogists thought that aside from misidentifications of aircraft lights, the genuine reports from Hessdalen were a novel phenomenon in the local atmosphere, and that the shape and structure being seen in some of them was 'read into' these blobs of energy through human expectations that UFOs were craft. Such an idea might have implications for many other UFO reports elsewhere.

In early 1982, after the wave of January and February was over, the Norwegian defence department sent two investigators to the region. They discovered that the lights had been seen for many years before 1981 but were rarely discussed.

In 1983, the UFO groups from three Scandinavian countries got together to launch Project Hessdalen. With donations from UFOlogists and a lot of skilful persuasion of various scientific institutes, they borrowed a terrific array of equipment, including a portable radar, lasers, magnetometers and seismographs to measure the minor earthquake activity in what was again found to be a heavily faulted region.

Braving the atrocious weather, a small team set up camp in a caravan within the valley for five weeks during January and February 1984. They were rewarded with 188 sightings in all. Many they identified in simple terms but several proved significant. They were able to obtain a battery of scientific readings gathered for each light, as well as photographs of what they saw on various occasions. They effectively proved that UFOs were real.

The most curious experience was at 6.12 p.m. on 20 February, when project member Leif Havik saw a small red light that appeared in the snow at his feet and moved all around him. It was not dissimilar to the laser light that they had for use on-site, but was not there on that day. On several other occasions they fired this laser at pulsing lights and in eight out of nine instances apparently provoked a response (e.g., a change in flashing sequence). This was one of several things during the study which suggested that the Hessdalen phenomenon might be more than just a natural energy source.

Later that year, a meteorological station set up temporary camp in the valley, taking numerous measurements and launching balloons to test the atmosphere. They concluded that there were real anomalies taking place but that these might relate both to freak mirage effects and to plasmas generated in the atmosphere by weather effects. This idea was not unlike the phenomenon being proposed at the same time by some scientists in Britain and Japan to try to explain the crop circles.

A year later a second expedition was mounted. The weather was much worse than previously and

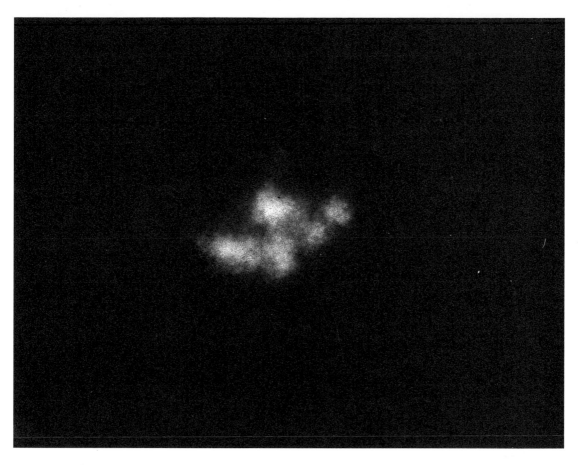

One of the photographs taken by observers in the remote Norwegian valley of Hessdalen. Although the phenomenon appears to be an unusual form of atmospheric event, and is here a series of unconnected glowing forms, it is easy to see how a witness would 'read' a shape into them and thus describe seeing a domed craft of some sort. Is this how many structured UFOs are 'perceived' amidst less substantial, but very real, sightings?

the sightings were fewer. The resources to mount the sort of experiments needed have not been available again – although a few brief private skywatches into the valley have been organized.

Sightings continue. On 18 February 1985 at Tynset, just south of the valley, with the temperatures even colder than the Hessdalen skywatchers had to endure, a mother collecting some family post spotted a strange oval object which had vertical stripes down its side – coloured red, green and orange. It also had a slight fin on each end. The woman brought her three children outside and they all watched as it drifted over the valley, swaying from side to side and twice projecting a searchlight beam towards the ground. This sighting resembles the airship reports of the nineteenth century.

The Hessdalen valley is far from an ideal place to organize a skywatch, especially between December and February, when sightings peak but the long dark nights and weather can offer their worst. However, if you wish, try to work with UFO Norway in planning this endeavour. Better still, also attempt to provide the sort of equipment that such an exercise really needs. After all, UFOs have been proven to exist in Hessdalen beyond any real doubt. What we need to know now is exactly what they are. For that, rather more than perseverence and dedicated observation is required.

United Kingdom

Although only a small group of islands off the mainland of northern Europe, the United Kingdom is densely populated and laden with UFO tradition. We will look at the five key window areas here.

Luce Bay, Scotland

Situated in the extreme south-west of the country, with the main town of Stranraer at its hub, this is a rugged and lonely region which has long produced UFO reports.

Possibly the most famous occurred on 4 April 1957, when the RAF base at West Freugh detected an object on radar. It was said to have been, 'too fast, too big and too manoeuvrable' to be an aircraft and turned through various acute angles in flight. This makes a mockery of the later official explanation that it was a weather balloon released near Belfast in Northern Ireland. Base commander – Wing Commander Walter Whitworth – admitted that 'there is no question of the radar playing tricks'.

In 1988 the files on the incident were declassified under the British government's 'thirty-year rule', allowing a clear picture of what really happened to be seen for the first time. In fact, there were several UFOs, all of which moved at speeds far in excess of weather balloons and changed course so completely that they flew against the wind for most of the time. All secret attempts to explain them failed and the balloon solution is now seen to have been a hasty cover-up to hide their unknown status.

This was by no means the only time UFOs appeared in the area. In October 1955, a buzzing saucer-shaped object flew over a van on a lonely road near Newton Stewart, an area with a history of odd magnetic or radio anomalies. The van engine failed at close proximity to the UFO.

On 23 and 24 January 1979, there was a series of encounters in the Stranraer area with what

seems to have been the same object. Described as a grey cigar with portholes emitting either green or orange light and carrying a red pulsing light, it silently circled the hills then flew out into the bay. Similar waves followed in late 1981 and early 1982.

Another frequent sight in the area is the orange oval. This appeared to three Ministry of Defence police officers at RAF West Freugh at three-thirty a.m. on 12 October 1980, before flying off over the sea.

Every spot here has hills and most have sea views, which offers quite a few locations to sky-watch. Stranraer can be reached by train or ferry boat.

Lothian, Scotland

Moving north and east up country the Lothian region surrounds Edinburgh and, whilst less active than Luce Bay (possibly due to being more heavily built up), has brought some exciting encounters.

Undoubtedly the best known is the famous UFO landing at Livingston, then a new town development west of the city. This occurred on the morning of 9 November 1979, amidst a whole wave of UFO sightings in the area. A forestry worker in Dechmont woods, north of the town, came upon a strange object on the ground inside a clearing. It was semi-transparent – as if fading out of reality. He was 'attacked' by two round spheres with spikes on the edges, which emerged from the object and floated towards him. He smelt an odd odour and recovered some time later on the ground, weak and suffering effects akin to anaesthesia. The UFO was gone and some feel that his dog had scared it away. However, strange marks were left on the ground at the site, which were quickly roped off for a police investigation, and the witness himself had tear marks on his trousers.

An extensive investigation was conducted by BUFORA (British UFO Research Association), which found nothing odd in soil or trouser samples but failed to uncover any evidence against the witness's sincerity. Many ideas – from ball lightning to hallucinations – were suggested, but the case remains a classic in Scottish UFO history.

Livingston was visited by another daylight UFO on 17 November 1978, when a silver disc was seen to rise from the forest and then sink back into the trees when spotted by girls at a nearby school.

Adjacent Broxburn has also figured commonly. In August 1973 there was a series of cases where car engines failed in the presence of UFOs.

Another likely location to look for UFOs is to the east of Edinburgh at Tranent. There have been spectacular cases here. On 2 February 1979, a disclike craft appeared and tilted to project a beam of light towards the ground. The beam mysteriously cut off in mid-air, as if it were solid.

A contact case took place in the area on 16 February 1980, when a man claims that several small creatures wearing silver suits emerged from a hovering oval, which emitted a smell of burning sulphur. One of the beings uttered demonically, 'This was once our planet and if you do not change your ways we will have to send a warning and only the chosen will be saved.'

Edinburgh has charming old buildings and scenery and is probably one of the most delightful cities to base a skywatch, compensating admirably if you see nothing. But you may well be wise to concentrate on the Livingston area. On 11 August 1991, a triangle was reported in the skies over the Bathgate Hills and it was seen to project beams of light towards the ground. Seconds later an explosion rocked a house at Blackridge.

The local UFO research team will offer guidance on skywatching but the site of the 1979 landing near Dechmont has now been commemorated by a plaque installed there by the local council. Oddly, this credits noted UFO debunker Arthur C. Clarke, merely because the case featured (as did many others) on the TV series made in his name. This ignores all the hard work put into establishing the story's credibility by those who investigated it. That decision aside, this makes the landing site part of a very exclusive club. It is certainly the only such spot in Europe, possibly in the world.

South-West Dyfed, Wales

Wales has a long record of strange lights. Two northern sites are noteworthy. Around Harlech there have been several waves which, in 1905, were attributed to a religious revivalist movement by media sources. More recently, the area inland from Rhyl and in the hills around Denbigh and Mold has triggered countless strange encounters – notably an incident in April 1984 when the military invaded the hilly village of Llangernyw in Clwyd, after locals saw a purple, oval mass drop to earth in the night.

However, possibly the most favoured spot is the rural coastlands to the south and west of Milford Haven, where in February 1977 one of the biggest UFO waves ever experienced in Britain took place and became the subject of no fewer than three books (probably a record for any single window area).

It began with sightings of a silver object *on* the ground near a Broad Haven school. As most of the original witnesses were children the story created a lot of attention, but there were some doubts about an unusual farm machine being the cause. However, one of the witnesses was the son of an RAF squadron leader at RAF Brawdy, a local NATO base. His testimony was thought credible by his father.

Although these and quite a few of the well-publicized cases were later demoted in significance by investigators, the publicity brought many new reports from witnesses who might have otherwise remained silent.

Typical was the case on 17 March 1977, when a family were driving from Dale towards Broad Haven, west of Haverford West. A glowing yellow ball followed the car, which lost both its engine and lights for a time.

There were also encounters with entities. In the early hours of 19 April, an oval object landed in a field at Little Haven and some figures wearing white plastic suits, described as tall with long, gangling

▲ Typical of the lights seen at Warminster in Wiltshire and at many other UFO-haunted areas. This was taken by UFO investigator Ian Mrzyglod in 1976. Warminster has many artificial stimuli, such as army flares and searchlights or military helicopters.

▶ In August 1980 some circles appeared in a field of oats near Westbury in Wiltshire. Nobody saw them form. The puzzled farmer reported them and investigations were begun by local UFO investigators, headed by Ian Mrzyglod of west-country group PROBE, and meteorologist and physicist Dr Terence Meaden. The swirled circle with flattened edges was then remarkable, but was soon to become a common site throughout Wessex in summer months.

arms, were seen to inspect an underground nuclear bomb shelter.

The lanes which criss-cross the coastal area are narrow and dangerous at night. The cliff-top paths offer spectacular views in daytime but extreme care is needed in the dark. For a time there were claims of a UFO base on Stack Rock, a little outcrop off the coast, west of Talbenny. This was triggered by reports of UFOs seen flying 'into' the bird-infested crevices. Even more bizzare allegations about underground tunnels linking here to the NATO base

followed. In truth, these seem little more than folk-lore, but do at least provide a focus for a skywatch.

Warminster, Wiltshire

During the 1960s, the name Warminster became synonymous with UFOs around the world. The country town is on the edge of the Salisbury Plain, noted for its ancient monuments such as Stonehenge. But it is also a busy military training ground with helicopters, ground manouevres, para-chute flares, searchlight beams and much else to keep the skywatcher alert.

Local journalist Arthur Shuttlewood wrote a whole series of books about odd goings-on in this region, some seventy miles south-west of London, after the 'Warminster thing' became celebrated following 1965 sightings. Because many of the encoun-ters involved an orange ball of light that rolled across the sky it became more popularly known as the 'amber gambler'.

103

Opinion is divided as to how many circles are hoaxed. Many certainly have been exposed or admitted as such. Before the major publicity drive of 1989 only about one hundred (maximum) were found each summer. Since then many times that number and with ever more complex formations have appeared. Some researchers, thus, say that most of these recent complex patterns could be fakes, with the real circles much simpler and relatively few in number. Always assume a circle may be hoaxed unless proven otherwise. One clue to look for is a bare hole in the centre where a pole may have been inserted so that a rope or chain could be tethered and swept around to flatten the circle. That was the case here at this Mansfield, Nottinghamshire hoax in July 1989.

This is the home of the skywatch. During the hippy days of the late Sixties, the surrounding hills were rarely without UFO watchers and local barns still sport UFO graffiti. New Age hippies also still congregate here.

Typical of the reports was a sighting on 8 October 1965, when the ever-present orange ball approached a car, whose engine failed and lights flickered like a candle. A dark mass was then seen by the woman driving the car, as it departed, leaving a trail of sparks through the air.

Aside from visual observations many people in this part of Wiltshire have suffered difficulties with their cars over the years. There are persistent stories of humming or buzzing noises and violent winds from nowhere shaking vehicles on quiet roads. There are also reports of strange swirled areas of crop which may connect with the 'thing'; although they were usually found without any known cause or were seen to form without any visible stimulus laying down the stems. One account describes a classic circle being marked out like a lady's fan opening up in the field.

Given this social context it is not surprising that the region around Warminster is now the focus of the crop-circle phenomenon, with hundreds being

found around the town or a little further south into Hampshire every single summer. In one sense, this seems to be caused by a phenomenon of unknown origin, which has always existed in the area and continues to create strange crop marks even today. But on the other hand, the area has also attracted many tricksters through the years, who now hoax crop circles. They may well place them here because it is where everybody is looking – so why not! It also ties them in with UFOs because of the Warminster heritage.

In 1992, it was admitted to BUFORA that one of the most famous photographs of the Warminster 'thing' which created much of the national and then international media attention was, in fact, faked.

Certainly, this is a fine place to skywatch and during the crop-circle months of May to August you will probably not be on your own. Hills such as Cradle Hill and Cley Hill near Warminster are favoured viewing positions. If no UFOs appear, the military activity should hone your IFO-spotting skills.

Occasionally hoaxers who get on to farmer's land by stealth can be clever. They can follow 'tramlines' left by tractors so as not to create footprints, enter by less obvious routes to fool investigators, and make efforts to cover up holes left by incriminating poles. That was the case in this July 1990 ring at Lower Peover in Cheshire. Holes that were covered up by loose crop were found on careful inspection at the centre. Most other researchers pronounced this case undeniably real!

The Pennine Hills

Researcher Paul Devereux believes that there are good reasons why these various British locations are major UFO windows. He has isolated many faultlines passing through the local rocks in each one and feels that these areas appear as obvious candidates for his 'earthlights' theory. This says that energies generated by forces in the rocks create UFOs.

By far the most significant location emerging from these studies is the Pennine Hills on the Lancashire-Yorkshire border, in a triangle of high moorland between Leeds, Manchester and Sheffield. Indeed, this has proved undeniably to be Britain's most consistent UFO hotspot.

Project Pennine, an investigative team involving Devereux, his 'earthlight' scientists, and northern UFO researchers such as Andy Roberts and David Clarke, has traced an extensive history of sightings of strange lights that stretch far back into the history books. Often they were associated with witchcraft or demons, by the people who first saw them. At Longendale, on the valley road east of Manchester, there is a sharp bend known as the 'Devil's

► The split in the boot of police officer Alan Godfrey after his Pennine encounter with a hovering UFO at Todmorden, West Yorkshire in November 1980. He lost ten minutes of time, and under later hypnosis told a typical abduction story of alleged medical examination.

◄ The bleak facade of Pendle Hill near Burnley in Lancashire. Once the haunt of witches, it has seen several close encounters with UFOs.

Elbow' where a strange light has been seen for centuries (hence the name). Further north near Burnley is the infamous Pendle Hill, where witches were rolled down in barrels to test their powers. If they survived their guilt was assured.

Today, the light phenomena that are still seen in these same areas are, of course, given very different interpretations. In 1914, one of the best British airship reports occurred over Pendle Hill. On 9 March 1977, when two factory workers were driving nearby at 3.10 a.m., a multi-coloured, humming object fell out of clouds above the hill, stalling their car engine and cutting out their lights, terrifying the two men with a heavy static-electric force that pressed down on their heads, making their skin tingle, eyes water and hair stand on end. It is very easy to see how such cases would have been interpreted in previous centuries.

The hills also have a very high concentration of close encounters and UFO abductions. The most famous is the missing ten minutes endured by police officer Alan Godfrey after seeing a rotating oval

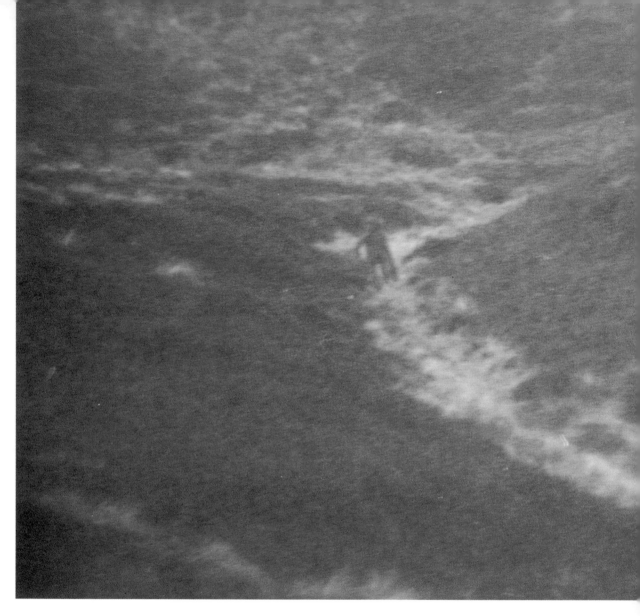

mass from his patrol car when on duty on the outskirts of Todmorden in November 1980. The object even left a 'swirled circle' on the wet road surface at this point. This seems identical to the crop circles left in cereal fields elsewhere.

But there have been plenty of other sightings which have achieved less media attention, many of them highly regarded by UFO researchers. Although UFOs can be seen from almost any good vantage point in this region, it is worth bearing a few tips in mind.

By far the most interesting encounters occur between midnight and dawn, especially around three a.m. Also, the metropolitan conurbations that dominate the region are not the best places to look – although the moors immediately outside both Oldham and Rochdale have provoked many impressive encounters, including a spate of police patrol chases of the so-called 'mystery helicopter', which was actually a typical ball-of-light UFO.

The hills to the north of Leeds, especially around Ilkley, have had their fair share of encounters and various ideal spots to skywatch can also be found on one of the several trans-Pennine routes between Manchester and Sheffield, where the desolate surroundings are enhanced by the presence of large reservoirs, well known to be triggers for UFO activity.

▲ A remarkable Pennine window photograph – literally a little green man! The photographer was a seemingly credible former police officer crossing the moors near Ilkley, West Yorkshire early one morning in December 1987 when the figure appeared. He took one photograph before it ran behind a bluff, got into a disc-like craft and vanished skyward. The witness has insisted on anonymity and has made no money from his photograph.

The witness was examined by a clinical psychologist and hypnotically regressed – and an 'abduction' memory emerged. The photograph has been pronounced genuine by several analysts, including research at the Kodak laboratories. It shows a figure approximately four and a half feet tall, but no analysis can tell us whether this is a real alien, a mock-up based on a dummy or a prankster in a costume.

▲ Occasionally an image appears on a photograph out of nowhere which is very mysterious. This picture of his daughter was taken by a Cumbrian firefighter. He saw nothing at the time, but upon development what looks like a figure in a space suit appeared behind the girl's head. All attempts to explain it have failed. It seems not to be a double exposure.

A witness in the Rossendale Valley of the Pennine window describes a disc-like object that he saw rise from a quarry at Stacksteads, near Bacup, in February 1979.

However, the best location of all based on recent sightings numbers seems to be the Rossendale valley on the county border – stretching in a narrow strip from Rawtenstall in Lancashire over the Yorkshire border towards Todmorden. A staggering array of close encounters has been reported in this small zone – including a UFO beneath a reservoir at Helmshore, everything from odd lights to a landing with a time lapse close by another reservoir at Weir, firey earthlights over the moors near Bacup,

and several abduction, entity and time-loss cases in and around Todmorden itself.

Some UFOlogists say that the best place to look is a disused quarry at the small valley community of Stacksteads, just west of Bacup. It has had some remarkable stories, but I am a little worried by that fact. You see, I was actually born and raised in Stacksteads and its status as a major window area gives me the rather un-nerving feeling that UFOs have been following me around ever since!

Part III Gathering the Evidence
5 CIRCLE WATCHING

MYSTERIOUS SWIRLED circles have formed in crop fields for many years. They were first reported in numbers in Queensland, Australia, in the mid-Sixties, but also appeared in the Warminster, England, area at about the same time. They were linked with UFOs because to some they looked like marks we might expect from a landed 'saucer'. Also, both areas where they appeared are UFO windows where sightings are common. Nevertheless, most of the time they were simply found in fields by puzzled farmers. UFOs were not seen.

We now know that swirled circles appear in historical records; we found them in fields as early as the sixteenth century. Nevertheless, they do seem to have become more widespread since about 1980, when a few were discovered near Warminster and a national, then international, search began.

Totals increased almost every year after that. At first, this seemed due to the greater media interest as more people were looking for them (especially from the air, from which they are far easier to spot). However, by 1988, there were dozens found each summer – including some outside the Wessex

One of the best known crop watchers came onto the scene some time after serious UFO researchers such as Ian Mrzyglod and scientists like Terence Meaden, but Colin Andrews – here – was the author of the best-selling book *Circular Evidence* in 1989 (along with colleague Pat Delgado). Andrews seems to feel that unknown energy forces and possible other intelligences are behind the circles, disputing the views of most scientists and key researchers at UFO group BUFORA that they are hoaxes and weather effects.

111

After *Circular Evidence* was published the media took to crop circles in a big way and the debate about their origin generates hundreds of stories every summer. This is rather like the way in which the UFO phenomenon hit the headlines forty years earlier, and many see fascinating sociological parallels between the development of the two subjects.

counties (Hampshire and Wiltshire), even a few outside Britain altogether.

Nine out of ten remained simple, single areas of crop that were swirled flat without the stems being broken and with the edges of the untouched crop remarkably erect. They did look supernatural, as if a biscuit-cutter had descended from the sky and stamped out the pattern. But they were not obviously the product of an alien Intelligence.

UFO experts rejected alien landings, pointing out that nobody ever saw this happen. A group of scientists led by Dr Terence Meaden and supported by BUFORA developed a theory that rotating air in

Dr Terence Meaden has developed a theory that is backed by scientists from around the world. This argues that the circles are the result of an electrical vortex corkscrewing down from the sky. Surprising support has also come from Britain's major UFO group, BUFORA. Several of its key officers have endorsed the theory as a possible solution to puzzling UFO reports. Here Dr Meaden and BUFORA researcher Paul Fuller undertake a joint investigation at a circle site in Wiltshire.

As well as simple, single-crop circles of various sizes (which form about ninety per cent of all known cases) crop rings are also known. The cereal in a ring is flattened in a circular band with the central part unaffected. These are much less common, but a typical example was researched by Robert Moore in Somerset in August 1991.

the lee of hills could spin like a tornado and corkscrew down on to a field. A strong electrified component may also be present and ionize the air to produce a glowing spinning top mass which, if seen, would naturally be interpreted as a UFO.

The theory made great sense – until the summer of 1989, when everything changed. Several crop-circle groups were now being set up to try to establish that circles were the result of an Intelligence using unknown forces to convey a message (often viewed as being somehow ecological). A best-selling book by circle watchers Colin Andrews and Pat Delgado set the tone and, as if in response, the circles became even more complex in design and totals multiplied to several hundred a year in Britain alone. All varieties of circles, rings, dumbells and later even highly graphic 'pictograms' were formed, leaving the door open for assorted attempts to decode their meaning, and a whole new industry of crop-circle watchers. They rapidly became more widespread than the UFO movement, which had spawned the subject.

Of course, many thought that the two phenomena were inter-linked – that the circles were the latest communication by the UFO Intelligences was an often-heard suggestion. Those who had supported the electrified-air vortex theory proposed that this natural energy also created many puzzling UFO

Part of the evidence for Dr Meaden's theory comes in the proximity of many circles to the lee slopes of a hill, which he argues facilitate the formation of his novel atmospheric phenomenon. A typical crop circle at Upton Scudamore, Wiltshire in July 1990 shows this relationship.

Investigating a circle site can be a complex business. At a massive circle formation near Warminster, in Wiltshire, July 1990, a scientific team uses equipment such as geiger-counters to check for any anomalies.

sightings, even if no circles formed. They pointed to cases such as the Alan Godfrey 'abduction' at Todmorden. This may show that circles could appear in any environment. Here a wet road was the temporary medium. Other cases in snow, sand and grass were also known. It just appeared that crop fields were ideal because they retained the marks for a long time. Once laid down, the crop stayed deformed for days or weeks, probably until harvested. Circles elsewhere normally vanish within hours and long before anyone finds them.

The war of words was compromised by many hoaxers, who faked circle patterns (often complex shapes). Some even alleged they made *all* or most of the circles as a joke. The vortex theorists supported them, saying that there were very few real circles and *all* these were simple patterns. The rest were fakes triggered by the publicity. Other researchers disagreed.

If you want to take the study of crop circles further, then there are details of where to seek help in our Further Reading section at the back of the book (see page 140). There are sound reasons for believing that UFO windows may be good places to look. If you visit a good hill overlooking crop fields on a leeward slope, some researchers say you will maximize your chances. But if you intend to go into a field it is essential that you get permission. Crop circles do little damage to the field and the crop can still be harvested. Careless sight-seers wandering in to inspect the patterns can lose farmers a great deal of money and so they are rightly very angry about unauthorized entry.

The best thing to do is try to document the

Although many crop circles are undoubtedly faked as a result of the publicity, researchers believe that the swirl patterns are sometimes so complex that only non-mechanical rotational forces can lay the plant stems with such precision. This is the complicated interlacing of crop found inside a circle at Preston Brook, Cheshire in August 1990. This formed alongside both strange sounds and lights reported in the dead of night and in an area that has a long and extensive record of UFO close encounters, notably car stop incidents – precisely as the Warminster area does.

In some instances the hoax is self-evident. Few would claim that the smiling face patterns which formed in Wiltshire in the summer of 1990 are anything other than a trivial hoax . . . although one or two did try!

formation of the circle in detail. About thirty eye-witnesses have described how they saw a circle form, but good visual observations are always needed. Because real circles appear very quickly and most during the early hours of the morning (even the hoax ones!), it is difficult to film them in creation. If you have access to video cameras – or a still camera loaded with film that can 'see' in the dark and take photographs of a suspect field every few minutes throughout the night – this could prove an ideal way to seek new evidence.

Of course, this kind of research can be time-consuming and expensive. If your presence is announced to locals you might even attract tricksters.

Both the scientific and the more esoteric-minded crop-circle watchers mount some sort of site monitor in southern England each summer and there is scope to organize similar ventures elsewhere. Joining one of these projects may be the best way to help out – without the prohibitive costs. Or, of course, you can just watch, wait and hope at a likely site, where you might be lucky. At least you can gaze from a hillside to record the beauty of circles that have already formed.

If you really want to see the circles, the best view is from the air. This can be expensive unless you join with a few friends to charter a light aircraft. In Wessex, airfields such as Thruxton should allow you to do that.

There is a great deal still to be learnt about crop circles and new ideas for projects are always appreciated by the main research teams. To date most effort has gone into simple watches, loaded with cameras and the taking of samples from the soil and crop at circles already formed. More needs to be done to record various factors, such as temperature, local barometric pressure, magnetic fields – in fact, almost anything – at the times before, during and after circle formation. This is very much a research field for pioneers and anyone has the ability to contribute.

Provided you are sensible, respect landowners and the country code and work with a recognized crop-circle group, wherever possible, you should have a fascinating time. But do make the effort to acquaint yourself with what we know about hoaxing. Follow our tips for how to spot them. Trickery is rampant, as is to be expected given the public interest. Everyone can be caught out but the combination of care, common sense and a realistic approach will stand you in good stead. Work on the basis that a circle is most likely to be hoaxed until evidence says otherwise, that it's not real unless proven.

The very complex 'pictogram' shapes are all considered suspect by some serious researchers. Others hail them as proof of an intelligent message. But it is a fact that the historical precedents traced for circles to date are all simple circle formations. None are pictograms. Also, none of the eye-witness claims of seeing circles under formation involve a pictogram either. These patterns *only* appeared after the major publicity of 1989 first brought to the fore the 'unknown intelligence' theory.

6 PHOTOGRAPHING UFOS

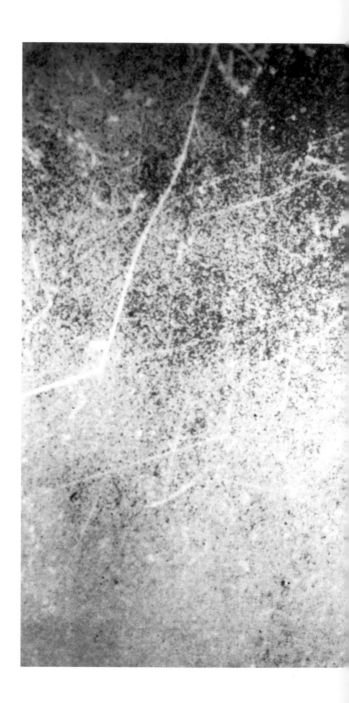

IF YOU go to one of the UFO hotspots recommended in this book, or mount a skywatch at a crop-circle site, what should you do if something strange appears? Obviously, photograph it – which is easier said than done!

In this book you have seen many of the best UFO photographs that have ever been taken (plus a few that do not deserve such description). Although camera ownership has increased dramatically and film quality has improved significantly there are now less UFO photographs submitted to investigators than there were decades ago. Why is this? By all expectations we should be swamped with impressive photographs of sharply focused and well-defined objects. With but a few exceptions, often suspect, we are not.

In recent years many people have started to use sophisticated camcorders. A few video clips of UFOs have been submitted as a result (none of which have as yet proven to be unexplained or particularly impressive). But the number of ordinary UFO photographs is at an all-time low.

One problem is that UFOs tend to appear at night, when few people are about with their cameras or using film that could successfully record an object in such dim conditions. This is why being properly equipped on a skywatch is so important. The use of low-light film and a camera which allows you to vary the shutter speed is a must.

Also, many photographs of UFOs have no background scenery such as trees or houses – which offer perspective and make analysis much more

A UFO photographed over South America? Still thought genuine by many, it illustrates another clue to look for in UFO pictures. The dark rim around the object is an indication that this is a small object close to the camera. If it is a UFO it is one about the same size as a car hubcab.

120

In July 1952 there was a major wave of sightings over Washington DC. A later photograph submitted to UFOlogists was said to capture the formation of lights hovering over the Capitol building. But it merely shows one method of photographic investigation. The 'UFO fleet' is a flare from the street lamps at the base of the building bouncing internally off the camera lens. Such lens flares are common in dark shots containing bright lights.

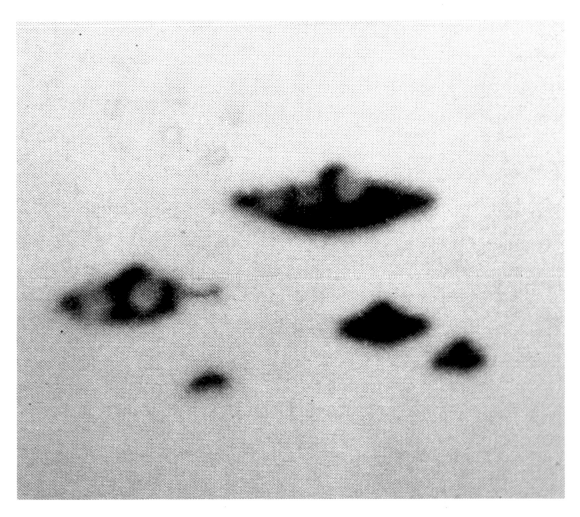

This photograph was taken by Alex Birch when a young boy. He said he snapped it in his South Yorkshire garden in 1962. For some years it was revered by UFOlogists but he later told how it was hoaxed, merely by filming the sky through a glass sheet on to which he had stuck the UFOs! Nowadays such a method would probably not fool UFO investigators.

useful. A shot of what may look like a marvellous disc against a blue sky is next to useless because it may be impossible to tell if it is a huge craft far in the distance – or a car hub cap, just a few feet in the air. The scale in a photograph is crucial. Look again at the McMinnville, or Williamette Pass photos and see now why they are considered so important.

More cynically, it might be argued that UFO photographs are less commonly submitted these days, as trickery is easier to spot. It may also not have the same lucrative aspect it once did, as media sources are less likely to feature UFO pictures without question, as once they might have.

In 1962, when UFO group BUFORA was first formed in Britain, a schoolboy, Alex Birch, was invited to show some photographs he took in his South Yorkshire garden. They created a storm, were featured uncritically in the media and even the Ministry of Defence took him just as seriously. Years later he admitted that he had faked them in a very simple manner, putting a few dark blobs on to a sheet of glass and shooting the sky through this to create an effective illusion. As nobody was

A classic disc over Madrid in Spain was taken seriously for many years. Computer enhancement of the image shows what some say is evidence of a string holding up a small model. Certainly the case is now less valuable than it once was thanks to more sophisticated UFO-investigation techniques.

Another problem photo, taken near Rochdale in the Pennine Window in 1975. The photographer was a policeman. Is the shape of this UFO bird or crescent? Or is it a domelike object not dissimilar to the policeman's helmet? Judge for yourself.

looking for hoaxes in 1962, the photographs were accepted as proof of what everybody wanted to see.

A quarter of a century later, someone else tried the same trick on BUFORA, this time using colour film and snapping the sky through a window pane. This briefly fooled some UFO experts, but most investigators were now too cautious to be conned. They have developed careful techniques to test such images and the nature of the hoax was revealed upon analysis.

Of course, in today's world of special-effects, very clever hoaxing using double exposure or super-imposition of negatives can generate exciting

results and be very hard to identify. For this reason photographs are not treated with the reverence they once were.

When NASA sent deep-space probes to planets such as Jupiter or Saturn, they could not return the camera. A technique had to be devised whereby the image was turned into an electronic signal and reconstructed back on earth by computer. This same technique can also enhance pictures, changing the light and shade, and revealing surprising details that were hidden (e.g., string holding up models). Computer-processing of UFO photographs is expensive and few laboratories will devote time and money to assist, but where it has been used it has

Many UFO photographs show an object that just 'appeared' on the print when developed and was not seen when the picture was taken. Although it is possible that a UFO may zoom by without being noticed, most such photographs turn out to be faults on the negative, or processing blemishes.

demolished some highly respected cases. Others (such as McMinnville and Trindade Island) have passed the test.

But the most common type of UFO picture comes with the explanation that it just 'turned up' on the photographs when they were developed. The witness saw nothing when taking the picture. This is immediately suspicious. Almost always the photograph turns out to be a processing fault or a bird frozen in a UFO-like pose by the fast shutter speed. These days, a picture is usually only taken very seriously if supported by strong witness testimony.

126

7 UFO RECOGNITION

The Six Most Common Types of UFO

The amber gambler

⊡ DESCRIPTION. A small but distinct ball of light, larger than star- or point-sized, and usually orange, yellow or red in colour. Often seen near the horizon or close to ground level. Visible from a few seconds to minutes.

⊡ LOCATION. The most common type of UFO, found in most window areas. Responsible for almost twenty-two per cent of UFO cases. The name derives from Warminster in England, where it was seen regularly during the 1960s. However, it has appeared all over the world – notably at Marfa, Texas in America, and Hessdalen in Norway. Pay particular attention near power lines, where the amber gambler often hovers above the wires.

⊡ IFO OPTIONS. Occasionally, amber gamblers might result from optical mirages associated with the sun. At night, and if stationary, beware the possibility of the moon shining through cloud or mist. Many scientists think that ball lightning could take this form. This is a rare meteorological effect that mostly appears during thunderstorms, but not exclusively so. It is visible for seconds only and floats freely near ground level. Parachute flares are another common source near military bases.

A typical amber gambler. This is a still from a movie film taken by Peter Day at Cuddington on the Oxfordshire Buckinghamshire border in January 1973. A US Air Force jet crashed that morning and it is possible that this is burning fuel ejected from the stricken plane, but the case has received extensive investigation and is still considered a genuine mystery by some investigators.

◀ The flying football UFO. This was taken in Cumbria above an area where crop circles formed that month (July 1977).

▶ The cigar tube, as photographed by George Adamski. Its authenticity is open to some dispute, but many similar reports have been made.

⊡ WHAT IS IT? Considered too small to be a piloted craft, most researchers feel this is probably an as-yet-unknown natural energy phenomenon of an electrical nature, induced by earth forces or atmospheric ionization.

The flying football

⊡ DESCRIPTION. An egg or oval object shaped like an American football or rugby ball. It can be seen both at day or night. During the night it takes on a variety of colours. White is common, as is deep red or yellow, but a surprising number are an unusual deep blue or purple colour which can hurt the eyes to look at, suggesting the emission of light in the ultra-violet and infra-red spectrum. By day, they are often dull grey or translucent white. Usually in view for several minutes, rarely longer. Vehicle interference, physical illness effects and energy emissions (such as buzzing sounds) are common.

⊡ LOCATION. Seen at all major window areas and responsible for fourteen per cent of UFO cases. Seems to be particularly fond of motor vehicles, as if attracted to their metal bodies. Many of the sightings occur late at night or around two or three a.m. As a result, lonely roads, near bridges and isolated metal structures or power stations, are common spots for the flying football to manifest.

⊡ IFO OPTIONS. Ball lightning may again be a possibility, but more often in daylight the toy balloon is a common source of misidentification. These will usually drift very slowly, whereas the flying football tends to hover and then move away extremely fast or disappear on the spot (with or without sound or a flash of light).

⊡ WHAT IS IT? Again, most UFO experts favour a natural phenomenon; windows and structure are rarely seen and its high energy emissions seem unlikely to support occupants. Amongst the most scientifically intriguing of all phenomena. Meteorologists and atmospheric physicists take note.

The cigar tube

⊡ DESCRIPTION. A long cigar-like object or cylinder, common in daytime where it is widely said to be silvery, or like polished metal. Often reported with a line of windows or portholes and not uncommonly with a jet of flame from the rear. Usually visible for several minutes, sometimes longer.

⊡ LOCATION. Responsible for about sixteen per cent of UFO cases, it is less usual at window areas (although it does appear there) and is more likely to be seen at random, almost anywhere. Frequently high in the sky and rarely with any effects on people or vehicles. Can be seen in association with other UFO types – emitting objects or even detritus such as 'angel hair', or allowing UFOs to enter its body. As such is sometimes called a 'mother ship' UFO.

⊡ IFO OPTIONS. The most likely source of mistaken identity is the aircraft body reflecting strong sunlight. This can make the wings invisible to the eye, creating just a cigar or cylinder. Airships, blimps and dirigibles seen from the right angle are another possibility. At night (or rarely in daytime), satellite re-entries form a chain of burning debris which can be linked together by the mind to seem like lighted windows on an unseen but perceived shape of a cigar tube. Flames from the burn-up may also be seen.

⊡ WHAT IS IT? If the UFO status is real and the structure not 'read in' to a more amorphous mass, many UFO investigators think these may be craft of unknown origin. Some say they are larger parent craft, out of which smaller saucer-shaped objects emerge. More cautious UFO researchers find this improbable and suggest that the cigar tube is just an extreme of the flying football, possibly resulting from gravitational-rotation effects or line-of-sight vision.

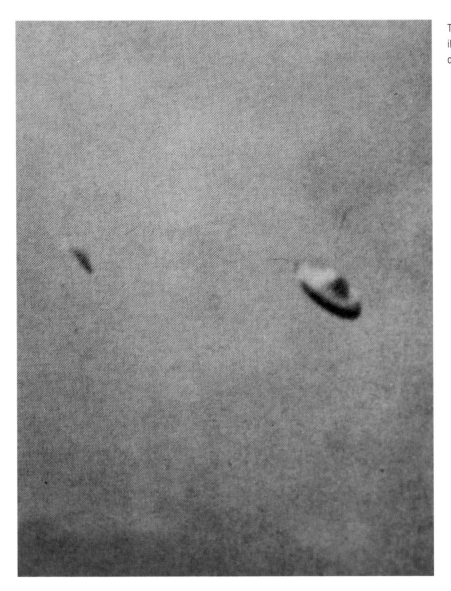

The upturned plate is illustrated by this UFO seen over Peru.

The Upturned Plate

⊡ DESCRIPTION. Usually resembles a large dish turned upside down, so that the base is flat and the upper part is domed. Can have a turret or light on top and may have lights inset into the base, but often simply a dark mass which emits no light. Seen as a metallic object during the daytime, or demarked by rotating circle of lights on the base at night. More common in daytime and difficult to see accurately at night, where the shape has to be interpreted against a darkened background.

⊡ LOCATION. Particularly common in North and South America, where it features in most window areas. Less so elsewhere but does appear and is responsible for about eight per cent of all UFO cases. More widespread in earlier years than today. Hardly any post–1970 photographs exist. The Pennine window in England has had several sightings with the tripod formation of 'balls' on the underside, as reported forty years ago by George Adamski in the USA. Usually seen at a distance, especially over mountains – rarely close. Lands in a high percentage of cases.

130

⊡ IFO OPTIONS. Aircraft are the most common source of misidentification, particularly at night when the saucer shape is assumed in a series of lights. When seen at an odd angle, or when involved with an advertising aircraft or blimp, the deliberate slow motion and lack of sound (from quiet or throttled back engines) can be deceptive.

⊡ WHAT IS IT? If the UFO identification seems certain and particularly when clearly seen in daylight, the possibility of a structured craft of some sort is considered high in these cases. Get a photograph! There has to be the option of a secret military device (such as a remotely piloted drone or a new form of airship) but these are among the most difficult of UFO cases to successfully explain in anything other than alien terms. But they are now rare.

The Saturn shape

⊡ DESCRIPTION. So called because it resembles the planet Saturn, with a central rim or ring separating two hemispherical domes placed one on top of the other. A common daylight type where it is usually said to be dark or silvery metallic in appearance. Less often seen at night, but if so then said to emit light from the inside (e.g., as in house lights) in many cases.

⊡ LOCATION. Comes nearer to ground level than the upturned plate and has been involved in a few close encounters involving vehicle interference, witness effects or time loss. Often seen to hover and rotate in those cases. Responsible for about eleven per cent of UFO reports. Seen in all areas, but quite common over or near water.

A classic example of the Saturn-shaped UFO is one of a series of photographs taken from a scientific survey vessel moored off Trindade Island in the Atlantic. The fuzziness was a real effect, possibly an ionization field, and the ship's electrical equipment malfunctioned as the UFO passed by.

⊡ IFO OPTIONS. Because of their hovering mode or slow drifting motion they can sometimes be balloons whose shape may be slightly distorted. UFO researcher Steuart Campbell has suggested that this UFO type could on occasion be a double mirage effect when near ground level.

⊡ WHAT IS IT? Although again widely viewed as a structured craft because of its seemingly artificial design, those crop-circle researchers who propose an electrical-vortex solution think that these UFOs might be visual accounts of that same phenomenon. They suggest that the rotating air sucks in dust to give the fuzzy appearance often reported on the edge of these Saturn-shaped objects. They do commonly rotate, as these scientists say their vortex would, and the buzzing sounds, electrical discharges and glows on the rim that are also reported would be consistent with the theory. If true, it is a previously unknown and very rare natural phenomenon which is highly energized and potentially dangerous.

The triangle

⊡ DESCRIPTION. A triangle or conical object. In the daytime, usually seen as a silvery or dark mass,

moving slowly and visible for many minutes. More common at night as three lights in a triangular formation. Colours vary.

⊡ LOCATION. Has been quite rare, accounting for just eight per cent of UFO cases, but waves have occurred in African and central European windows. The recent wave in Belgium has followed on similar short bursts in the Hudson Valley, north of New York (which occurred in the mid-1980s) and longer waves in central England (around Cheshire, Staffordshire and Leicestershire). Seen at all heights, including near ground level, but very rarely actually on the ground itself. Far more common at night.

⊡ IFO OPTIONS. In daylight these can commonly be balloons, as noted by their slow movement and very long duration. Triangle UFOs are seen for a few minutes only. At night aircraft lights when flying directly towards you (such as a Lockheed Tristar with a high tail-light) can appear like this.

⊡ WHAT IS IT? Many feel it may be a new type of secret Stealth aircraft.

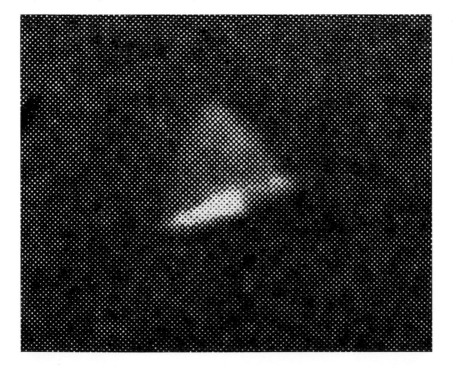

The triangle UFO type resembles a high-flying balloon (as here).

8 YOU ARE NOT ALONE

Famous Witnesses to UFO Events

MILLIONS OF people have seen UFOs, and that means all sorts of people ranging from politicians to housewives and astronomers. These include some very well-known celebrities. Three of their experiences are described here and might help you come to terms with your own encounter. If you do experience something then at least you will know that you are not alone.

MICHAEL BENTINE, COMEDIAN
'Where there's Foo . . .'

Towards the end of the Second World War, the now famed entertainer and former member of the comedy team 'the Goons' was an Intelligence officer with the bomber wing of 626 Squadron. He told me what happened after a raid on the secret Nazi weapons base at Peenemunde:

Three or four crews came back with identical stories that they had been pursued by a light which was pulsating and had flown round the aircraft. So I said, 'You mean St Elmo's fire?' But they said, 'No, no, no. We've all seen that.' As far as they were concerned it was some sort of weapon. So I said, 'What did it do to you?' And they said, 'Nothing.'

So I said it was not a very effective weapon! Then another crew came in, then another. And in the end it was obvious that these people had seen it. About forty-eight hours later an American officer came in. He'd been going around the group

and he said, 'I understand your crews have seen it . . . we call them 'Foo fighters' and they appear in daylight as well. We don't know what they are.' So I said, 'No, neither do I and nor do the aircrew.' That was probably the manifestation of what is now called a UFO.

JOHN LENNON, MUSICIAN
'There are UFOs over New York'

The former member of the Beatles had a close encounter one night, when he was with TV soap actress May Pang. It was 23 August 1974 and they were in John's penthouse flat overlooking New York City. John was naked on the terrace (seemingly not unusual), when he called May out to see an object like a flattened dome with a bright red light on top and a circle of white lights on the underside. It flew past the United Nations building – where four years later a debate on UFOs was held – then directly above the balcony without making any sound.

Lennon was fascinated by UFOs and read a lot about them, including the UK magazine *Flying Saucer Review*, whose illustrious readers also include members of the Royal family. Lennon included a cryptic note about the UFO sighting on his *Walls and Bridges* album, and in one of his last songs before his murder in 1980, ('Strange days indeed') he said, 'There's UFOs over New York and I ain't too surprised.' Now you know why.

Many other musicians have had UFO encounters. The group Hot Chocolate reached number one with their single 'No doubt about it', describing their encounter, and the Carpenters even recorded an anthem for an international 'contact' day entitled 'Calling Occupants of Interplanetary Craft'.

WILLIAM SHATNER, ACTOR
'Captain Kirk Rescued by Aliens?'

This headline may not be as ridiculous as it seems, because Canadian actor Shatner, who played the captain of the Starship Enterprise in the 'Star Trek' television series and more recent movies had a remarkable escape when he drove out on his motorcycle into the blistering heat of California's Mojave

Desert. He stopped briefly for some water and his friends rode on, leaving him alone to catch them up later. But to his horror the motorbike engine had failed and he was stranded miles from anywhere. Unless he found civilization quickly, the searing heat would claim another victim.

Escape depended on choosing the right direction to walk towards safety. If he went the wrong way he might not find aid until too late. He set off and then had a sudden urge to change direction. At the same time, overhead, he caught sight of a strange silvery object that was streaking through the air – a UFO. He trusted his new judgement, found help in time and was rescued. But he always wondered if he might not have someone out of this world to thank.

Scottish rock band CE IV have had several UFO experiences and now write music about the subject. They perform on stage with their own alien, and have recorded an eerie album based on what it is like to undergo an abduction (available via 81 Ryeside Road, Glasgow, Scotland G21 3LG).

9 WHAT TO DO IF YOU SPOT A UFO

If You See a UFO?

Making a record

Make an immediate sketch of what you saw and write down as many details as you can recall, paying special attention to the information on pages 36–7. Ensure that you record the date, time and exact location of the sighting (giving a map reference, if possible) so that this is not forgotten. It may prove to be of importance.

If you can get other witnesses, this greatly enhances the value of the sighting. Take their names and addresses and ask them to write out their account as soon as possible, agreeing to send copies to one person who will collect and forward them to an investigating source. But do *not* discuss the sighting in detail with each other until after such notes have been written.

If you have been able to take a photograph, follow the advice on pages 37–9, and take comparative photographs at the site in daylight.

If you feel confident that what you have seen is not likely to be an IFO (see pages 120–26), then you can call the local police, airports or air bases. This may put your mind at rest, but it is unlikely they will have time to do more than perhaps recommend you to a UFO group. Ask for advice on this. Police and air bases in most countries (e.g. Britain and Australia) have a facility for making an official report on your behalf via the Defence Minis-

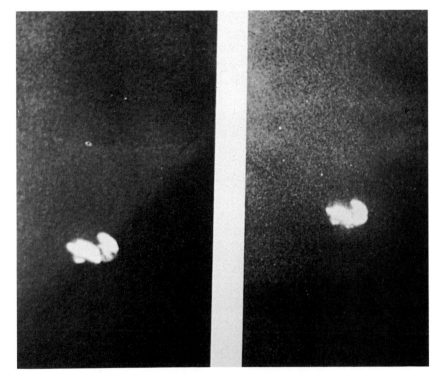

Witnesses can be extremely reliable and intelligent people. In his book, *The UFO Experience*, Dr J. Allen Hynek featured two photographs of an as-yet-unexplained phenomenon, taken from an aircraft flying at thirty thousand feet. He said he could 'absolutely vouch' for their authenticity. Dr Hynek later explained to me why this was so and I agree. I can vouch for them, too!

Studies have also noted that witnesses are of above-average intelligence and tend to be gifted in artistic creativity and visual perception. This skilled artist depicts some of her own extensive UFO visions in a way that well illustrates the point.

try. Your sighting will be logged on a data base, but do not expect to receive any reply concerning this record, as the investigation carried out will be minimal and you will almost certainly not be informed of any results.

Telling others
This can be the most daunting experience. There is a great fear of being laughed at or even of losing credibility with friends or employers.

Remember that you are not alone. UFOs have been seen by millions. Tell cynics that you have the company of US President Jimmy Carter, the astronomer who discovered the planet Pluto (Clyde Tombaugh), top USAF consultant Dr. J. Allen Hynek, and countless other highly intelligent people. UFOs have been seriously debated in the American congress, the British parliament and House of Lords, and American Association for the Advancement of Science and the United Nations.

The French equivalent of NASA has spent millions of Francs following up cases, and their Minister of Defence has admitted that baffling and unsolved reports still remain. Similar statements have come from top government figures around the world.

If people want to laugh at you, tell them to ponder these facts before they do so. They may see that they are the ones out of step – not you.

A good idea is to stress that you accept that more than nine out of ten UFO sightings turn out to have simple explanations and you are *not* stating that what you saw must be an alien spaceship. All you are seeking is an explanation – if possible – for what you saw in the sky, or to document details for posterity and scientific analysis if no obvious answer is found. Who can honestly chastise you for that? There are many fascinating things up there to be seen. If you just happened to see one of them, then it was you who had your eyes open. Others merely failed to pay attention!

You can also throw some facts and figures at these people. Studies carried out by psychologists working with UFO witnesses have all found that they tend to be of *above-average* intelligence, highly observant and with excellent visual creativity.

If you want to discover more about the UFO subject I have prepared a selected bibliography for you. Most libraries stock UFO titles, but do not just read and accept everything you come across. This is a very contentious subject and there are many strange theories and a lot of nonsense. Little is proven beyond doubt. Nobody yet knows what is going on. So if you cannot find the books on this list at your library or bookstore, ask for them to be ordered for you. I also give details of specialist booksellers where you can purchase the best UFO titles by mail order as soon as they appear.

There are many UFO groups and the ones listed here are all considered reputable. If you ask them to deal with you in confidence, they will do so. As none have any outside funding (all operate strictly on voluntary efforts and membership subscriptions) it always helps if you can afford to send them a stamped self-addressed envelope (SAE) or an international reply coupon.

Self-policing is difficult in a field where anyone can claim to be a UFO expert without qualifications, but the British UFO Research Association (BUFORA) and the Australian Centre for UFO Studies (ACUFOS) operate a code of practice to regulate the behaviour of their investigators when dealing with witnesses. Although other groups have as yet been unwilling to follow this, BUFORA have recently made the code mandatory for all members when they join the group. So, if you do have a complaint about the way you are treated, channel this through either group and they will try to help.

UFOs have been seen by millions of people worldwide. Although more than nine out of ten sightings turn out to have simple explanations, there still remains that crucial percentage which remains a mystery.

If all else fails, or you simply want to share an experience with me, then I will gladly help out if I can and treat the matter in confidence, if preferred. You can write to me care of:

37 Heathbank Road,
Cheadle Heath
Stockport
Cheshire SK3 0UP
United Kingdom

Have I seen anything?

This is a fair question. The answer is yes. I have seen about ten things that would be reported as a UFO by most people. One of them was repoted to a newspaper by another witness as a 'dome shape' hovering over farmland in Lancashire. I was asked by a journalist who did not know that I was a UFOlo-gist what I had seen. I told him it was a peculiar yellow light that hovered low on the horizon. Only my awareness of the subject and on-site investi-gation had revealed that it was a helicopter with a searchlight on top that was flying up and down a field in my line of sight whilst it was crop spraying. This was so far away no sound was heard.

I have seen other IFOs by training myself to watch the sky, but in September 1980 near the Avebury stone circle in Wiltshire I did see three unusual lights form a triangle, then wink out. This has yet to be explained.

UFOs are one of the most exciting mysteries of the modern world. You can play your own part in responding to the puzzles. I hope this book will help you in that quest. But do remember: *Keep your feet on the ground as you keep your eyes on the skies.*

Further Reading

Most titles are given as first editions. Many have subsequent overseas and paperback editions available. Only English-language originals are listed.

General

Anatomy of a Phenomenon, by Jacques Vallée. Regnery, 1965.

Challenge to Science, by Jacques Vallée. Regnery, 1966

The Scientific Study of UFOs, by Edward Condon (Ed). Bantam, 1969.

The Humanoids, by Charles Bowen (Ed). Spearman, 1969.

UFOs: A Scientific Debate, by Sagan & Page (Ed). Cornell, 1972.

The UFO Experience, by Dr J. Allen Hynek. Regnery, 1972.

UFOs Exist, by Paris Flammonde. Putnam, 1976.

Encounter Cases from FSR, by Charles Bowen (Ed). Signet, 1977.

The UFO Conspiracy, by Jenny Randles. Blandford, 1987.

UFOs: 1947 to 1987, by Evans & Spencer (Ed). Fortean Tomes, 1987.

Phenomenon, by Evans & Spencer (Ed). Futura, 1988.

History

The Report on UFOs, by Edward Ruppelt. Doubleday, 1955.

The UFO Controversy in America, by David Jacobs. IUP, 1973.

The Roswell Incident, by Berlitz & Moore. Grafton, 1980.

The Great Airship Mystery, by Dan Cohen. Dodd Mead, 1981.

Clear Intent, by Fawcett & Greenwood. Prentice, 1984.

Science and the UFOs, by Randles & Warrington. Blackwell, 1985.

The UFO Encyclopaedia (3 Vols), by Jerome Clark (Ed). Apogee, 1990 and 1992.

UFO Crash at Roswell, by Randle & Schmitt. Avon, 1991.

Investigations

The UFO Evidence, by Richard Hall (Ed). NICAP, 1964.

The Interrupted Journey, by John Fuller. Dial, 1966.

The UFO Handbook, by Allen Hendry. Doubleday, 1979.

UFO Study, by Jenny Randles. Hale, 1981.

Project Identification, by Harley Rutledge. Prentice, 1981.

Missing Time, by Budd Hopkins. Marek, 1981.

Confrontations, by Jacques Vallee. Ballantine, 1990.

From Out of the Blue, by Jenny Randles. Berkley, 1993.

Window area studies

The Truth about Flying Saucers, by Aimé Michel. Criterion, 1956.

The Warminster Mystery, by Arthur Shuttlewood. Spearman, 1967.

The Dyfed Enigma, by Randall Jones-Pugh. Faber, 1978.

Close Encounters Australian kind, by Keith Basterfield. Reed, 1981.

UFOs – African Encounters, by Cynthia Hinde. Gemini, 1982.

The Pennine UFO Mystery, by Jenny Randles. Grafton, 1983.

Project Hessdalen, by Erling Strand (Ed). UFO Norge, 1984.

Night Siege, by Hynek & Imbrogno. Ballantine, 1987.

The Tujunga Canyon Contacts, by Druffel & Rogo. Signet, 1989.

The Gulf Breeze Sightings, by Francis & Francis. Morrow, 1990.

Theories

Flying Saucers: A Modern Myth, by Carl Jung. Routledge, 1959.

Operation Trojan Horse, by John Keel. Putnam, 1970.

UFO Phenomena and Behavioural Science, by Richard Haines (Ed). Scarecrow, 1979.

UFOs: The Public Deceived, by Philip Klass. Prometheus, 1983.

Visions, Apparitions, Alien Visitors, by Hilary Evans. Aquarian, 1984.

The Earthlights Revelation, by Paul Devereux.
  Blandford, 1989.
Mind Monsters, by Jenny Randles. Aquarian, 1990.
Revelations, by Jacques Vallée. Ballantine, 1991.
Secret Life, by David Jacobs. Schuster, 1992.
The Omega Project, by Dr Kenneth Ring, Morrow,
  1992.

Crop circles
Crop Circles: A Mystery Solved? by Randles &
  Fuller, Hale, 1990.
The Crop Circle Enigma, by Ralph Noyes (Ed).
  Bartholomew, 1990.
Circles from the Skies, by Terence Meaden (Ed).
  Souvenir, 1991.

Book availability
Try the following specialist mail-order services for
old and new UFO titles:

Arcturus Books
PO Box 831383
Stone Mountain
GA 30083–0023
USA

Lionel Beer Books
115 Hollybush Lane
Hampton
Middlesex TW12 2QY
England

Brigantia Books
84 Elland Road
Brighouse
Yorkshire HD6 2QR
England

Specialist Knowledge
20 Paul Street
Frome
Somerset BA11 1DX
England

Susanne Stebbing
41 Terminus Drive
Beltinge
Herne Bay CT6 6PR
England

Sydney Esoteric
475–9 Elizabeth Street
Surry Hills
NSW 2010
Australia

Magazines
Most UFO groups listed below issue publications.
Although there are excellent magazines in French,
Spanish, and Italian in particular, recommended
ones to look out for in English are:
UFOs: UFO Times (BUFORA)
International UFO Reporter (CUFOS)
MUFON Journal (MUFON)
Northern UFO News and UFO Brigantia (NUFON/
  IUN)
Enigmas (SPI)
UFO Afrinews (Cynthia Hinde)
Just Cause (CAUS)
NUFOC (NUFOC, Belgium)
UFORA Research Digest (UFORA, Australia)
The independent magazine *Flying Saucer Review* is
a rich store of cases, especially the older issues.
You can contact them at:
FSR Publications
PO Box 12
Snodland
Kent ME6 5JZ
United Kingdom
Crop circle journals include:
Journal of Meteorology (TORRO)
The Crop Watcher (CERES)
The Circular (CCCS)

Worldwide Organizations

Africa
Cynthia Hinde
Box MP 49
Mt Pleasant
Harare Zimbabwe
Africa

North America
CUFOS
(Center for UFO Studies)
2457 West Peterson
  Avenue
Chicago, Illinois
IL 60659, USA
CAUS
(Citizens Against UFO
  Secrecy)
PO Box 218
Coventry, Connecticut
CT 06238, USA
MUFON
(Mutual UFO Network)
103 Oldtowne Road
Seguin, Texas
TX 78155–4099
USA
CUFORN
(Canadian UFO Research
  Network)
Box 15
Station A
Willowdale, Ontario
M2N 5S7, Canada
UFORIC
(UFO Research and
  Investigation Centre,
  Canada)
Dept 25
1665 Robson Street
Vancouver,
British Columbia
V6G 3C2, Canada

South America
CADIU
Cassila de Correo 218
Cordoba
Argentina
SBEDV
CP 16–017
Correio do largo do
  Machado Rio
Brazil

Australia
UFORA
(UFO Research Australia)
PO Box 229
Prospect, South Australia
5082

Europe
SOBEPS
74 Avenue Paul Janson
B–1070 Brussels
Belgium
SVL
Oever 28
B–2000 Antwerp
Belgium
NUFOC
Jodenstraat 66/102
B–3800 St Truiden
Belgium
AESV
BP 324
13611 Aix-en-Provence
France
CENAP
Eisenacherweg 16
D–6800 Mannheim 31
Germany
CISU
Corso Vittorio
Emanuelle 108

10121 Torino, Italy
UFO Norge
Boks 14
N–3133 Duken
Norway
V-J Ballester Olmos
Guardia Civil 9
D–16
46020 Valencia
Spain
AFU
PO Box 11027
S–60011 Norrkoping
Sweden

United Kingdom
BUFORA (British UFO
  Research Association
Suite 1
2C Leyton Road
Harpenden
Herts AL5 2TL
NUFON
(Northern UFO
  Network)
37 Heathbank Road
Stockport
Cheshire SK3 0UP
SPI
(Strange Phenomena
  Investigations)
41 The Braes

Tullibody, Alloa
Scotland FK10 2TT
SRUFO
(Scottish UFO Research)
129 Langton View
East Calder
West Lothian
Scotland EH53 0RE
CERES
(Circles Effect Research
  Society)
3 Selborne Court
Tavistock Close
Romsey
Hants SO51 7TY
CCCS
(Centre for Crop Circle
  Studies)
20 Paul Street
Frome
Somerset
BA11 1DX
TORRO
(Tornado and Storm
  Research Organization)
54 Frome Road
Bradford-on-Avon
Wiltshire BA15 1LD

In Britain you can tune in to weekly updated reports on all the latest news, sightings, lectures, books and activity in the UFO world through UFO CALL, a twenty-four-hour service offered by BUFORA, via the British Telecom network. As of Spring 1992, rates were thirty pence per minute off-peak.
Call 0891 121886

INDEX

142

Acronyms

ACUFOS	Australian Centre for UFO Studies
BUFORA	British UFO Research Association
CUFORN	Canadian UFO Research Network
CUFOS	Dr J. Allen Hynek Center for UFO Studies
CE IV	Close encounters of the fourth kind
FSR	Flying Saucer Review
FUFORG	Fylde UFO Research Group
GEPAN	Study group into novel atmospheric phenomena
IFO	Identified flying object
IURC	Irish UFO Research Centre
J. Met.	Journal of Meteorology
MIB	Men in Black
MIT	Massachusetts Institute of Technology
MoD	Ministry of defence
Oz Factor	UFO triggered altered state of consciousness
RPV	Remotely piloted vehicle
SOBEPS	Belgian UFO study group
UFORA	UFO Research Australia

Picture acknowledgements

The author and publisher would like to thank the following for the use of their photographs:

page 7, Zurich Library; 15, Fortean Picture Library; 19, A. P. Villa Jnr; 21, Stephen Darbishire; 22, Global Communications/Jim Dallmeier, 23, Dorothy Izatt; 28, 30, 37, NASA; 29, 42, Roy Sandbach; 31, Futami, Tokyo; 32, FUFORG, Lancs; 35, the Oldfields; 39 (top), IURC; 39 (bottom), 90 (bottom), Orbiter; 45, Peter Warrington; 48, BUFORA; 51, 99, Project Hessdalen; 54, Spanish Air Force; 59, 60, Paul Trent; Ella Fortune; 66, Carl Hart Jnr; 69, 89, 131, 135, CUFOS; 80, T. Nieuwenhuis; 83, Peter Horne/UFORA; 85, UFORA; 88, Jenny Randles/J. Met.; 95, Aime Michel; 102, Ian Mrzyglod; 108, Peter Hough; 109, Jim Templeton; 111, Paul Fuller; 114, Robert Moor; 123, Alex Birch; 125, MUFORA; 127, Peter Day; 134, CE IV; 136, Judith Starchild.

Every effort has been made to track down the copyright holders of the photographs in this book. However, given that the pictures are often many years old and are spread all around the world, this has not been possible in several cases. If we have failed to credit the correct copyright holder in any instance we would be delighted to set this matter right in future editions if the correct source is brought to our attention.